Modern Times

*The Biography of
a Hungarian-Jewish Family*

STEPHEN POGANY

BRANDRAM

First published in Great Britain in 2021
by Brandram, an imprint of Takeaway (Publishing)

1st KDP edition

Takeaway (Publishing), Chapel House, Exeter EX4 2AT

E-mail: books@takeawaypublishing.co.uk

British Library Cataloguing in Publication Data.
A catalogue record for this book is available from the British Library

Cover design by Nóra Váraljai

ISBN 978-0-9931896-4-7

For my late wife
Ruth Hazel Pogany
(1954–2007)

and for my late parents
Vera and George Pogany
(1926–2021 and 1928–2021)

Fragment

I lived on this earth at a time
When man was so debased
that he killed wantonly not just on command,
When rage-filled delusions
and crazed obsessions held him in their grip.
I lived on this earth at a time
When murderers, traitors and robbers
were acclaimed as heroes,
When base informers were deemed praiseworthy
and when those who remained silent and stood apart
were hated and shunned like plague victims.
I lived on this earth at a time
When anyone who dared to raise his voice had to go
into hiding
Chewing his fists in frustration and shame
As the country around him turned savage,
grinning drunkenly on blood and filth.

I lived on this earth at a time
When children cursed their mothers,
When women rejoiced if they miscarried
and when the living — glancing at the cup of foaming
poison that stood on their tables —
envied the maggot-infested cadavers lying in their
graves.
. . . .
. . . .
I lived on this earth at a time
when even the poet was silent,
waiting for Isaiah to speak out once more;
for only the prophet could utter an appropriate curse
no-one else could command such terrible words.
. . . .

1944

Miklós Radnóti

Contents

Part Three: The End of History

Acknowledgements

I began work on this book in 1998, putting it aside for lengthy periods to concentrate on academic projects, on semi-journalistic articles and, all too frequently, from a sense of hopelessness. I wanted to tell the story of a Hungarian-Jewish family — my family — drawing on the writings of historians and poets, social scientists and novelists, on interviews I'd conducted with relatives as well as with people I'd encountered in Hungary and Transylvanian Romania and, not least, on my grandmother's anecdotes about growing up in Budapest in the early years of the twentieth century. Somehow, my grandmother's stories, which were invariably about her parents and siblings and about her teenage hopes and ambitions, stopped abruptly before adulthood and her marriage to my grandfather.

From the very beginning, I felt that my family's story should be told in a 'voice' unencumbered by either academic jargon or sentimentality. I spent a decade looking for that voice. I found it, or at least an approximation, while working on assignments for a creative writing class that I attended in Leamington Spa. I am grateful to the tutor, Steve Calcutt, and to the members of the class for their unstinting encouragement and for sharing their own work with me.

My indomitable grandmother, Etelka Farago, died in 1977. However, both my mother, Vera Pogany, and my late uncle, Bert (Bertalan) Farago, patiently answered my many questions. The interviews I recorded with them, in Canada, the Netherlands, Britain and Hungary, form the basis of much of this book. I am also grateful to my cousin, Ági Friss, who shared memories of her father, Ágoston, a noted figure in Hungarian football from the 1920s onwards. Finally, I am indebted to Edit Salamon, a child survivor of the Holocaust. I have drawn on Edit's account of her extraordinary experiences in wartime Budapest in Chapter 16. Sadly, Edit passed away in March 2020.

Árpád Kajon and Tamás Pintér, historians associated with the excellent 'A Nagy Háború blog' ('The Great War Blog'), went to a great deal of trouble to respond to my queries about the military career of my paternal great uncle, Dezső Platschek, in World War One. Until they wrote to me with their detailed findings, I had no idea that my family contained a genuine war hero. I am also extremely grateful to Boglárka Bánusz and Orsolya Balogh of MTK Budapest, who provided me with a wealth of information about the many and exacting responsibilities assumed by my maternal great uncle, Ágoszton ('Ági') Weisz, with MTK and with the Hungarian Football Federation. I fear that Ágoszton would be dismayed by his great nephew's total lack of interest in his chosen sport.

Many people have read all or part of the manuscript and have offered valuable advice and encouragement. In addition to Steve Calcutt and the members of his creative writing class, I should like to thank Ditta Aydemir, Anne Cohen, Glyn Cousin, Roghieh Dehghan Zaklaki, Diana Elbourne, the late Robert Fine, Erika Harris, Éva Horváth, Ambreena Manji, Boldizsár Nagy, George and Vera Pogany, Irena Powell, Mihály Riszovannij, Esther Ronay, Pál Salamon and Ferenc Takács. Mihály Riszovannij's encylopaedic knowledge of Hungarian and Hungarian-Jewish history enabled me to correct several errors that appeared in an earlier draft of the manuscript, for which I am very grateful. Liam D'Arcy-Brown, my publisher, has been a pleasure to work with. His enthusiasm, profession-alism and painstaking attention to detail have contributed greatly to whatever merit this book may possess. My debt to Glyn Cousin is immense. Glyn helped to keep me on track,

Acknowledgements

both intellectually and emotionally, whenever the project seemed in danger of foundering.

This book is dedicated to my late wife, Ruth Hazel Pogany (1954–2007) and to my parents, the late George and Vera Pogany, who passed away in late spring 2021. When I produced a first tentative draft of the early chapters, my wife was warmly encouraging, although she came to despair at my sluggish rate of progress. Only a few lines from that initial draft have found their way into this book. However, I think she would be pleased, as well as surprised, that the project has finally been completed.

All translations from Hungarian, unless specifically indicated to the contrary, are mine, including passages from poems by two incomparable twentieth-century poets, Attila József and Miklós Radnóti.

Stephen Pogany
Budapest, June 2021

Note

I have adopted the international practice of placing the given name before the family name, although in Hungarian it is the other way round. In general, the text retains the original Hungarian words used for geographical designators, e.g. *utca* (street); *tér* (square); *út* (road); *körút* (boulevard); and *híd* (bridge).

WEISZ Family Tree

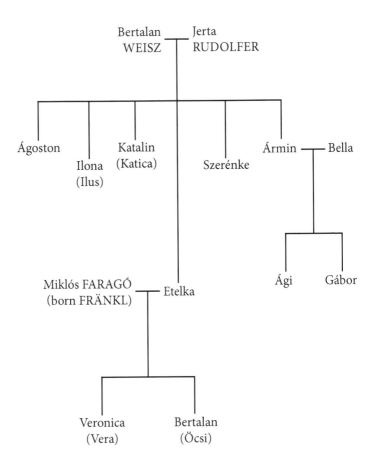

FARAGÓ (FRÄNKL) Family Tree

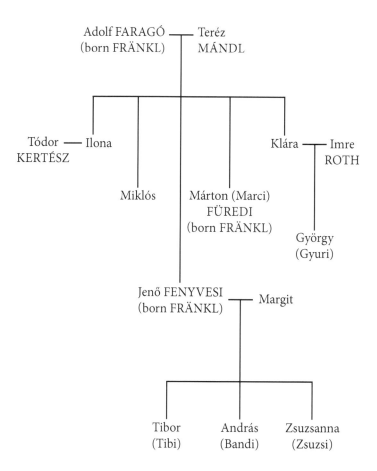

Adolf FARAGÓ (born FRÄNKL) — Teréz MÁNDL

Tódor KERTÉSZ — Ilona

Klára — Imre ROTH

Miklós

Márton (Marci) FÜREDI (born FRÄNKL)

György (Gyuri)

Jenő FENYVESI (born FRÄNKL) — Margit

Tibor (Tibi)   András (Bandi)   Zsuzsanna (Zsuzsi)

1

Prologue

If I had been more alert, I would have understood that, like some elaborately plotted detective story, my childhood was littered with clues. Sometimes, I asked the right questions, but I was too ready to accept the wrong answers. Without knowing it, I let my grandmother deceive me.

With my mother in Budapest, 1955

'Why do you eat that, *nagymama*?' I asked, pointing to the wafer-thin *matza* that Etelka broke into pieces before dunking in her milky, morning coffee. Shards of *matza*, as dry as the Kalahari Desert and as flavoursome as sawdust, could graze the inside of your mouth unless you took the precaution of moistening it first.

'Because I like the taste,' Etelka lied, confirming my opinion that adults are strange, lacking the good sense of children. Adults are children gone wrong.

On Friday nights, if my grandmother was staying with us in the north of England, she would surreptitiously light a candle in her room, disregarding my father's stern admonitions. Not without reason my father was afraid of being immolated while asleep in his bed, one of the hazards of sharing your home with an absent-minded old lady fond of candles. But my grandmother persisted, on the sly.

'Why do you light a candle, *nagymama*?'

'Out of respect for my parents.'

My grandmother's explanation, though not entirely truthful, was plausible. Etelka subscribed to a form of ancestor worship that, in its rigour and intensity, would have impressed the strictest Confucian.

If I had been older, or better informed, I might have understood the significance of my grandmother's behaviour. Just as I might have been able to comprehend the finality with which Etelka turned her back on Hungary after coming to Britain in 1958. Already past retirement age when she arrived in England, Etelka only returned to Hungary twice. At an age when many people take refuge in the past, my grandmother embraced the present, becoming an enthusiastic Londoner. After several years spent caring for one of her grandchildren in a south London suburb while her son and daughter-in-law went out to work, Etelka moved to a tiny, rented studio apartment in Bloomsbury with views over the park in Russell Square. From here Etelka ventured out each day to explore her adopted city.

My grandmother's urban expeditions were agonisingly slow and — for anyone accompanying her — acutely embarrassing. Pausing to ask a kindly stranger the way, Etelka would give every appearance of listening intently before stopping the very next person who came along and asking for directions once more, a process that she would repeat several times until she was finally satisfied. Frequently, the man or woman who had just explained the best route for my grandmother to take, often in painstaking detail, would still be standing there, a shocked spectator of Etelka's undisguised mistrust. Although they couldn't have known it, my grandmother's lack of confidence was indiscriminate. It encompassed the entire human race with the exception of certain members of her immediate family to whom she was bound by indissoluble ties of blood.

At the age of seventy, when her services as a childminder were no longer needed by her children, Etelka found employment as a relief typist in the Hungarian Department of the BBC World Service, helping to sow the seeds of discontent behind the Iron Curtain. Of course, Etelka had lied about her age to get the job.

Although my grandmother's relationship to the English language was never more than strained and uncomfortable, and although she talked interminably about her parents and her cosseted, upper middle-class childhood in Budapest, I was struck by the fact that she never showed much interest in revisiting Hungary. Unlike so many people who have left their homeland, for whatever reason, Etelka wasn't afflicted by nostalgia for the sights, sounds and scents of the country in which she'd spent most of her life. Despite her advancing years, my grandmother was an emigrant through and through, determined to put down roots in a new land.

Etelka's second and final visit to Hungary, in August 1973, was organised by her family. Accompanied by children and grandchildren, Etelka celebrated her 80th birthday in a comfortable rented villa, on the northern shores of Lake Balaton, during a relentlessly hot Hungarian summer. A few years earlier Etelka had visited Hungary alone, staying in a cheap hotel in Budapest and hardly seeing anyone. In an effort to save money, my grandmother had come close to starving herself, treating the modest hotel breakfasts, which were included in the price of the room, as virtually her only source of sustenance. Staving off hunger pangs in the evenings with bread rolls and crescent shaped *kiflis*, which she had kept back from her breakfast and which she ate in the privacy of her room, Etelka spent almost all of the money she had brought with her on a marble plaque for her father's tombstone.

The tombstone of Bertalan Weisz and of Szerénke

An older plaque, on the upper part of the tombstone, records the deaths of Etelka's father, Bertalan Weisz, of her youngest sister, Szerénke, and, in much smaller letters, of Etelka's mother, whose maiden name was Rudolfer. The stonemason has misspelt 'Rudolfer', rendering it as 'Rudoefer', but the mistake has been left uncorrected.

The circumstances in which Szerénke died, while still in her teens, remain shrouded in mystery. Depending on whom you talk to in the family, Etelka's youngest sister was killed in a fire at her place of work, succumbed to a lung infection, or became the hapless victim of falling furniture. However, Szerénke's parents, Bertalan and Jerta, died of natural causes when they were well into their seventies. The plaque is a record of private, familial grief of the kind you might find in graveyards almost anywhere.

The second and larger plaque on the tombstone, which was commissioned by Etelka during her brief, solitary visit to Budapest, commemorates the deaths of Etelka's husband Miklós, of her brother Ármin, and of Ármin's family, including his wife Bella and their teenage children, Gábor and Ági. None of the people on this second plaque died of natural causes. In every case they died unnatural deaths. 'To the memory of my martyrs', reads the inscription in Hungarian, without alluding to those responsible or the circumstances of their martyrdom. Adding such details to the plaque would have been costly as well as superfluous.

When I was an Afro-haired student at Edinburgh University in the early to mid 1970s, I often stayed with my grandmother on visits to London. One night, as I was erecting the rickety camp bed that almost filled the entire hallway of Etelka's studio apartment, my grandmother surprised me. '*Piszkos keresztények!*' Etelka exclaimed, without warning, from the adjoining room. 'Filthy Christians!'

My grandmother's outburst was both unexpected and disconcerting. Her words had no apparent connection with anything we had talked about that evening. Etelka had never expressed such rancorous sentiments before, at least in my hearing. Most of the people Etelka knew in Britain were Christians, if only nominally. In almost every case they had treated my grandmother with conspicuous kindness and generosity, going out of their way to be helpful and hospitable to this cranky and virtually penniless old woman with her limited and idiosyncratic grasp of English.

I was shocked and embarrassed by my grandmother's words. My partner, whom I was to marry the following year, had been raised as a Methodist. I myself had been baptised at the age of six in the local Congregational Church, in Cheshire, at the insistence of my parents. Who knew when a baptismal certificate, the ability to recite the Lord's Prayer from memory, or the presence of a foreskin might avert disaster?

Since leaving Hungary, after the 1956 uprising, my parents had set about erasing every trace of their Jewishness. They shunned the company of other Jews, preferring to make friends amongst their Christian neighbours and workmates. George and Vera, as my parents liked to be known, were convivial and seemingly open about their early lives in Hungary. They held frequent supper parties at which guests were served the hearty, coronary-inducing delights of the Hungarian kitchen — thick, meaty goulashes heavily seasoned with paprika, *Székelygulyás* in which fermented cabbage is stewed with pork (my parents had no inhibitions about consuming forbidden meat), *rakott krumpli* with succulent, moist layers of boiled potatoes, hard-boiled eggs, and spicy *kolbász* liberally doused in sour cream. And my personal favourite, *rakott palacsinta* — a shimmering tower of pancakes spread, alternately, with apricot jam and ground walnuts and topped with whipped cream. No one guessed that my hospitable, open-handed parents had anything to hide.

Yet even our family name was an exercise in dissimulation. My parents had assumed the name Pogány, which means 'pagan' in Hungarian, in 1950, two years after they were married in Budapest and fully two years before I was born. Previously, our family name had been Platschek, a common enough name amongst Ashkenazi Jews in Hungary and in the former Czechoslovakia. In choosing to call themselves Pogány, my parents were seeking to construct a new and less hazardous identity for themselves and their future children in Hungary. Of course, they couldn't have known that, within a few years, they would have the opportunity to leave Hungary and settle in Britain where their new name, just like the one it had replaced, would immediately brand them as foreign.

Although Etelka and I had always been close, I didn't challenge her intemperate language or ask her what she meant. Instead, I let her words drain away like water from an upset glass. It was only much later that I realised my grandmother must have been thinking about Miklós, her husband, who died on one of the so-called 'death marches' instituted by Hungary's pro-Nazi government in November 1944. Or perhaps she was recalling her diabetic brother, Ármin, who disappeared around the same time along with his wife and teenage children. All of them, together with literally dozens of other members of Etelka's extended family, were victims of what historians now label the Holocaust or *Shoah*.

For my grandmother, the Cross could never be a symbol of redemption or of Christian love, as I had been taught by my kindly, well-meaning teachers in Sunday school. For Etelka, it would always signify terror and random death. The gun-toting youths who had hustled my lame, war veteran grandfather away, in the winter of 1944, had worn armbands with the arrow-tipped cross of the Hungarian *Nyilaskeresztes* or 'Arrow Cross' Party.

Over time, I have tried to piece together the fragmentary clues from my childhood and to make sense of them. I have tried to make sense of the *senseless*. Almost without exception, my relatives had been hard-working, deeply patriotic people without wealth, privilege, or even conspicuous talent. In a word, my family had been ordinary.

No doubt there are distortions, omissions and inaccuracies in this narrative. By its very nature, a family memoir is bound to be selective and imperfect. It can only represent one point of view and, however meticulously researched, it cannot include every fact. This is as near as I've been able to come to the truth, or at least the truth as I understand it. This is what I think I know.

Part One

The Old Empire, 1856-1918

Previous page: Unidentified soldier (postcard, 1900)

2

Why photographs lie

In a photograph taken in Budapest in the early years of the twentieth century, my grandmother's father, Bertalan Weisz, is standing beside Jerta, his wife, a slight smile on his lips. To all outward appearances Bertalan and Jerta seem every inch a prosperous, middle-aged couple. Their solid, fleshy features and well-tailored, formal clothes convey an impression of sobriety and affluence. For the photograph, Bertalan is dressed in a dark jacket and matching waistcoat. A thick gold chain, connected to an unseen fob watch, hangs from the top buttonhole of his waistcoat. The heft of the chain hints at Bertalan's supposed wealth.

Beneath his waistcoat my great-grandfather is wearing a starched white shirt with one of those uncomfortable-looking wing collars; his broad silk tie has been fixed at a rakish angle. Bertalan's silver-flecked, walrus moustache bristles with manliness and pride and maybe just a hint of defiance. The jut of my great-grandfather's chin and the fierce gleam in his eyes suggests a character both resolute and peppery. Ejecting drunken or obstreperous customers from his bar, on Budapest's Jókai *tér*, wouldn't have posed a problem for him.

Next to her dapper husband, Jerta looks dowdy. Thickset, thin-lipped with plain, heavy features, her abundant brown hair is swept up into a bun. It's hard to imagine that my great-grandmother turned many heads, even in her prime. Dressed in a dark, elaborately embroidered silk dress, Jerta is wearing several pieces of jewellery including pendulous earrings, a large broach, and a thick gold necklace that reaches almost to her waist.

Like the portraits commissioned by merchants and landowners in earlier centuries, this photograph of my great-grandparents serves not only as a record of their physical appearance but also as a visual statement of their social standing and wealth. 'Just look at us!' the photograph seems to be saying. 'Don't you admire us and envy us?'

Only photographs can deceive. My great-grandparents weren't nearly as prosperous as they wished to appear. The bar was much less profitable than most people supposed, particularly after Bertalan had to find work in the family business for three of his adult children as well as a son-in-law. My great-grandfather struggled to pay their wages, while it's said that lack of funds prevented Bertalan from providing his daughters with the dowries that would have enabled them to marry well.

My great-grandfather's origins and childhood remain shrouded in mystery. According to his marriage certificate, in which his family name is recorded as Weiss rather than Weisz, Bertalan was born in Füzér, a tiny village in the remote northeast of Hungary. Bertalan was thirty-four years old at the time of his marriage, on 1 September 1886, which would mean that he was born in 1852, a fact confirmed by the inscription on his tombstone in Budapest.

In 1849, just a few years before my great-grandfather was born, Hungarians had conceded defeat after a long and bloody revolt against Austrian rule. Nowadays, a prominent street in every town and village in Hungary is named after Lajos Kossuth, Hungary's revolutionary leader, who died in exile in Italy. Kossuth's dream of resurrecting a sovereign, independent Hungary was shattered when, in a rare display of imperial solidarity, the Russian Tsar came to the aid of the Austrian Habsburg Emperor. Almost two hundred thousand Russian troops, supported by heavy artillery, overwhelmed Hungary's valiant but hopelessly outnumbered armies.[1]

In 1867, when my great-grandfather was fifteen years old, the fortunes of Hungary underwent another sea change. In an effort to shore up control of his fissiparous empire — with its squabbling Germans, Czechs, Hungarians, Croats, Poles, Romanians, Slovaks, Boyks, Slovenes and others — the Habsburg Emperor agreed to the formation of a Dual Monarchy in which Hungary would enjoy equal rights and status with Austria. Even though hot-headed Hungarian nationalists, including the exiled Kossuth, objected that this was a betrayal of the sacred cause of national sovereignty, most of their fellow countrymen were satisfied with the new constitutional settlement.

Under the terms of the *Ausgleich* or 'Compromise', which was approved by the Hungarian Diet and formally ratified by the Habsburg Emperor, foreign affairs, defence and the funding of the common government were the joint responsibility of Austria and Hungary.[2] However, in most other matters Hungary was granted full autonomy, although the Austrian monarch reserved the right to approve government-sponsored bills before they were introduced in the Hungarian legislature.

Until the ignominious peace treaty which Hungary's leaders were forced to sign after World War One — Austria-Hungary had allied itself with Germany in the War — the Kingdom of Hungary encompassed present-day Slovakia, Carpathian Ruthenia, Transylvania, Croatia, the Banat, and Vojvodina, *in addition to* the lands that make up Hungary today. For the duration of the Dual Monarchy, Hungary was considerably larger than either Great Britain or Italy, extending over 325,000 square kilometres.[3] If the *Ausgleich* failed to deliver full sovereignty, it allowed Hungarians to govern themselves — as well as several sizeable minorities — more or less as they pleased, within an overall territory that stretched from the Austrian border in the west to the remote *Székely* lands in the east, some 660 kilometres from the capital, Budapest.

The whereabouts of my great-grandfather Bertalan Weisz at the time of these momentous political events is unclear. According to my grandmother, her father was orphaned when he was eight or nine years old and, rather than going to live with relatives, he had run away to sea, finding employment as a cabin-boy on a merchant ship operating from one of the Empire's busy seaports on the Adriatic coast — Trieste, Pula, or Rijeka — places he would have known by their Hungarian names: Trieszt, Póla, and Fiume. However, it's far more likely that, following the untimely deaths of his parents, Bertalan went to live with relatives until he was old enough to strike out on his own, spending some years as a merchant seaman before marrying and settling in the Hungarian capital.

As for the circumstances in which Bertalan's father, Ármin Weisz, met his death, my grandmother always insisted that he was waylaid by robbers and murdered while travelling to a country fair to buy livestock. That sort of thing was common enough in the nineteenth century, particularly in the wilder parts of the Empire. Newspapers of the time are full of lurid accounts of robberies in remote places that ended in murder or grievous injury, and of smouldering grudges between *pálinka*-fuelled peasants, generally over women or land, that were settled with axes or cudgels. I have an entire file of such news items from a century and a half ago, culled from provincial newspapers. Take the case of Dumitru Tatalovics, a highwayman, who preyed on travellers in the Carpathian Mountains in the far northeast of the Empire. On 6 February 1886, *Máramarosi Lapok* informed its readers that Tatalovics had been sentenced to eleven years' imprisonment for three attempted murders and two robberies that he had carried out the previous year in the craggy Verchovina region. Nowadays, this bleak and remote area belongs to the Ukraine.

Like the hapless victims of the highwayman Tatalovics, my great-great-grandfather, Ármin Weisz, may have been surprised on a lonely country road at dead of night. From the newspaper account of Tatalovics' trial it seems that the highwayman was a poor shot, although he had no qualms about firing his pistol with deadly intent at innocent strangers.[4] *Máramarosi Lapok* reported that, around midnight on 6 September 1885, Tatalovics had emerged out of the darkness and fired at a passing cart carrying two brothers, Ábraham and Salamon Stern, and the carter. The Stern brothers fled in terror to a nearby inn where Ábraham discovered that the ball from Tatalovics' pistol had passed clean through his shirt without injuring him. Meanwhile the highwayman, who had been living rough in the local forests and who must have been running low on provisions, helped himself to the food that the carter was carrying.

Barely a week later, according to the same newspaper article, Tatalovics sprang out of bushes by the side of a road and pressed his pistol against the chest of a solitary wayfarer, Hers Czim, returning home on foot from Galicia. The highwayman demanded money but Czim attempted to flee. Tatalovics fired, missing his victim, but he caught up with Czim and dealt him a hefty blow on the back of the head with the butt of his pistol. As robberies go, Tatalovics' haul was meagre. He left the scene of the crime with Czim's hat and a one *forint* coin.

Like the victims of Dumitru Tatalovics my great-great-grandfather, Ármin Weisz, was a Jew. However, unlike the impecunious Hers Czim, he must have been carrying a substantial sum of money if he had been on his way to buy livestock at a fair, although the money belonged to his employer for whom Ármin worked as an estate manager. His assailant, if he had used a gun, must have been a better shot than the highwayman of Verchovina. In any event, whatever the true fate of my great-great-grandfather, Bertalan was left an orphan.

According to his marriage certificate, Bertalan was thirty-four years old and already living in Budapest when he and Jerta were married in September 1886. The certificate states that Bertalan was a *kiskereskedő* or 'small trader', a term that encompasses such activities as shopkeeping and running an inn. Bertalan's bride, who was ten years younger, had been living with her parents in Galgócz, which is also where the marriage was celebrated. Today Galgócz, more commonly known as Hlohovec, is a town in southwestern Slovakia.

Aside from the evidence furnished by the photograph and by their wedding certificate, there are only three things that I know about my great-grandmother. The first is that her mother tongue was German. Although Jerta learnt passable Hungarian and spoke Slovak with reasonable fluency, my grandmother always said that her mother preferred to speak German at home, lapsing into Slovak only when she wanted to discuss something in confidence with her husband.

The second fact that I know about Jerta, which I also gleaned from my grandmother, hints at a degree of gentility. Jerta exhorted her children to rise from the dinner table before they were sated. Such self-restraint, particularly in an age when many people often went hungry, suggests that Jerta came from a reasonably well-to-do family where lack of food was never an issue.

The third fact that I know about Jerta is that, like her husband, she was Jewish. The couple were married at the little synagogue in Galgócz. But my grandmother never said anything to suggest that either of her parents was particularly observant. For the most part, religion was worn lightly in my family, if it wasn't discarded altogether like a cumbersome layer of clothing that has become stifling in the heat of summer. If you had asked my relatives about their attitude to religion, I think they would have remarked that such things have their place but that they are no longer as important as they once were. My family liked to think of themselves as modern. Many of the younger members of my family, in particular, took little or no interest in religion, associating it with the musty, claustrophobic world of their ancestors, a place of impoverished villages, unpaved roads, unwashed linen and stifled ambitions.

My great-grandparents Bertalan and Jerta Weisz had six children. With the exception of Szerénke, who died when she was barely out of her teens, all of the children survived into adulthood. As for Ágoston, the younger of my grandmother's two brothers, he lived to be well over ninety years of age, a crumpled patriarch who ruled over his family with an iron will.

From the way she talked about her sister, it was obvious that my grandmother admired Szerénke, who was said to be beautiful and cultivated. Unlike Katica, another of the Weisz sisters, Szerénke almost certainly died a virgin, while much of her brief life was devoted to poetry. Szerénke's all-consuming desire was to become a poet and to achieve a measure of literary recognition. According to my grandmother, one of Szerénke's poems was published in a national newspaper, earning lavish praise from an eminent poet.

In my grandmother's account, which reads like the storyline of a rather sentimental Italian opera, Szerénke's untimely death occurred some years before the collapse of Austria-Hungary, when she was no more than seventeen or eighteen years of age: Szerénke, who had a delicate constitution, is said to have succumbed to a lung infection.

However, Ágoston remembered the death of his sister rather differently. In a handwritten account composed in old age, his description of Szerénke's death is more prosaic: furniture rather than consumption had carried away his sister. Ágoston was almost certain that an enormous bookcase had toppled forward onto Szerénke at the offices where she was employed as a secretary. But Ágoston admitted that he couldn't be entirely sure of the facts after the passage of so many years. If a rogue bookcase hadn't extinguished the life of his sister, Ágoston thought that Szerénke may have died in a fire that broke out in the building where she worked.

The precise circumstances of Szerénke's death are no longer important. However, it seems a pity that none of my great-aunt's poems has survived. What topics did my great-aunt write about? A lady poet of tender years and limited experience of the world, I imagine that she composed sentimental verses about nature and the passing seasons. But perhaps I'm misjudging my great-aunt? Maybe, in the privacy of her room, Szerénke was a blushing admirer of Endre Ady, the demonic and sensual young poet who took the Hungarian literary world by storm at the turn of the twentieth century with his bold, iconoclastic verses. 'I am the son of Gog and Magog,' begins the title poem of Ady's most celebrated book, published in 1906, bringing 'new songs for new times'.[5]

I don't know whether Szerénke ever experienced romantic love. If so, my grandmother never mentioned it. In literary terms, Szerénke's short life was like an unfinished novel that has barely progressed beyond a few brief introductory chapters. We will never know what would have become of Szerénke if she had lived to a decent age and if she had had the time to develop her talent. Maybe she would have found literary success and personal happiness. Perhaps her poems would have appeared in popular outlets like *Vasárnapi Újság*, (*Sunday Newspaper*), earning praise from leading poets of the day such as Mihály Babits, Milán Füst and Dezső Kosztolányi?[†]

In the years leading up to World War One, some of Hungary's most highly regarded women writers, including Margit Kaffka and Sarolta Lányi, published poems and short stories in *Vasárnapi Újság*, alongside Ady, Babits and others. Yet, although Lányi and my great-aunt would have been near contemporaries, and despite a shared passion for poetry, I doubt that Szerénke would have sought out Lányi's company or that Lányi would have found a kindred spirit in my great-aunt. Much like Endre Ady, Sarolta Lányi was an incorrigible revolutionary, appalled by the starkly inegali-

---

† I have not been able to discover any poems by Szerénke in Hungarian newspapers found in online databases of that era. However, a Szerénke Weisz, who may or may not have been my great aunt, is mentioned in *Budapesti Hírlap* on 6 March 1910. Szerénke, along with several other young people, took part in a well received concert organised by the Universal Circle, preceding a dance party that continued until late the following morning.

tarian society in which she found herself, with its multiple hypocrisies and injustices. By contrast, Szerénke, like her parents Bertalan and Jerta, was bourgeois, conventional and deeply conservative. Like almost everyone in the family, Szerénke abhorred radicalism and social upheavals of any kind. Aside from her attachment to the Dual Monarchy and to the sensible, orderly values embodied by Emperor Franz Josef, she kept well away from politics.

If Szerénke had still been alive in spring 1919, when a Soviet Republic was declared in Hungary, it's unlikely that she would have shared Lányi's unbridled enthusiasm for the new government headed by Béla Kun. There was little in Szerénke's upbringing or temperament that would have inclined her to celebrate the 'dictatorship of the proletariat' or the wholesale nationalization of factories, shops, restaurants and other businesses. After all, Szerénke's family owned a *kocsma* on Jókai *tér*, which provided an income for her parents and for several other close relatives.

Szerénke's untimely death, some years before the dissolution of Austria-Hungary, was a tragedy, both for her and for her grieving family. Yet even if my great-aunt hadn't died when she did it's far from certain that she would have lived to a ripe old age. Like Márta Sági, another Hungarian-Jewish poet, who committed suicide with her husband in 1944 to evade deportation to the Nazi camps,[6] the odds were stacked against Szerénke from the start.

3

How my great-great-grandfather Mika came to know the family of a famous Hollywood actor

Unlike the sepia photograph of my grandmother's parents, Bertalan and Jerta Weisz, I have no visual record of my maternal grandfather's family. Miklós' parents, Adolf and Teréz Fränkl, are shadowy and out of focus, forever indistinct. Yet, although I have no photograph, I possess two documents steeped in clues. These yellowing leaves of paper, clumsily held together with strips of adhesive tape, are my only tangible connection to Adolf and Teréz, both of whom died before I was born. From these documents, as well as from conversations with two of their grandchildren, I've been able to reconstruct a picture of Adolf and Teréz, at least up to a point.

Budapest's Dohány utca Synagogue, 1878

One of the documents is a copy of my great-grandparents' wedding certificate. Adolf and Teréz were married in Budapest on 20 August 1895. According to the certificate, the wedding took place at the Dohány Street Synagogue, a biographical detail that tells us quite a lot about them. Since its completion in 1859, the Dohány Street synagogue has been the largest and most important synagogue affiliated to Hungary's 'Neologue' movement, founded by Hungarian Jews in the nineteenth century as a progressive alternative to Orthodox Judaism.[7]

By marrying where they did, Adolf and Teréz were affirming their modernity and their broadly secular outlook. My great-grandparents didn't believe in *golems* or in pious, white-bearded rabbis with magical powers of healing and prophesy. Adolf and Teréz were practical, down-to-earth people; they took no interest in fairy tales. Adolf, who had trained as a typesetter in his hometown of Rózsahegy in present-day Slovakia, was eager to go into business. Like most of Hungary's Jews, Adolf looked forward to the twentieth century and to the opportunities that it was bound to bring.

Well, you shouldn't blame my great-grandfather for being an optimist. In those days plenty of people, including many of the country's leading intellectuals, believed that mankind moves relentlessly forwards and upwards in a perpetual quest for justice and enlightenment, rather than in a series of terrifying loops like a fairground rollercoaster. Who knows — if Hungary had been on the winning side in World War One, and if the country had escaped the ravages of the Great Depression, maybe Adolf's optimism would have been justified?

Naturally, there were plenty of Jews with a very different outlook to my great-grandparents. By the end of the nineteenth century, huge rifts had opened up amongst the

Jews of Eastern Europe. In Hungary alone there were the rival Neologue and Orthodox movements, as well as the ultra-orthodox *Haredim*, and the Status Quo faction.[8] There were also tens of thousands of Jews who were intent on eradicating all traces of their Jewishness, whether by marrying gentiles, converting to Christianity, or embracing a secular theology such as Marxism. A comparatively small number of the region's Jews, infused with the nationalist fervour gripping the peoples around them — Hungarians, Slovaks, Czechs, Poles, Romanians, Serbs, Croats, Slovenians, Ruthenians and others — became ardent Zionists. They adopted the ideas championed by the Austro-Hungarian journalist and political visionary Theodore Herzl, who believed that only the creation of a Jewish state on the parched land of their forefathers could offer the Jewish people security and salvation. All of these factions, secular and religious alike, as well as a constellation of splinter groups, were constantly squabbling with one another as well as amongst themselves.

If my great-grandparents, Adolf and Teréz, represented the progressive, integrationist tendency amongst Hungary's Jews, who saw themselves as Hungarians of the Jewish faith, the ultra-orthodox *Haredim*, in their broad-brimmed hats and black frock coats, lay at the opposite end of the theological spectrum. These sweaty, self-mortifying Jews, whose heartlands lay in the mud-clogged towns and villages of Polish Russia and in the remote northeastern provinces of Austria-Hungary, were determined to remain faithful to the old traditions and the old ways, whatever the cost. For the *Haredim*, being Jewish defined their whole lives. It dictated how they prayed, what they wore, what they ate and drank, whom they associated with and even the kinds of work they did. Their notion of Jewishness determined the language they spoke at home with their families, the cramped *cheders* to which they sent their sons, as well as their insistence on keeping their daughters at home in a state of divinely ordained ignorance, helping their mothers with the housework. The *Haredim* were mortally afraid that if their children received a modern, secular education they could be irredeemably contaminated by such subjects as physics, chemistry, or geography.

A Synagogue Courtyard,
Máramarossziget, 1907

The *Haredim* bore ostracism and insults with pride. It wasn't persecution they feared so much as freedom. If Jews were no longer forced to live a life apart, if they were free to set up home wherever they wished, to marry whomsoever they pleased, to study at any institution of their choosing and to take up any profession or calling, then the invisible bonds that had held Jewish communities together over so many centuries in the diaspora would surely unravel. The *Haredim* understood that emancipation would wreak more havoc than any number of pogroms or trumped-up charges accusing Jews of the ritual murder of Christian children. Emancipation offered Jews the possibility of surrendering the sacred burden of their Jewishness.

For the *Haredim*, religion was even supposed to define their lovemaking, although sex has a way of overcoming even the staunchest theological barriers. Take the Austro-Hungarian town of Máramarossziget, now the Romanian town of Sighetul Marmaţiei, in the lee of the Carpathian Mountains.

At the turn of the twentieth century, Sighetul Marmaţiei, now commonly known as Sighet, was one of the centres of Ultra-Orthodox Judaism, although you'd be hard put to find more than a handful of Jews living there now. In the early 1900s, Sighet was full of synagogues and prayer halls, of bearded, black-frocked Jews huddled at street corners, discussing the finer points of the *Mishnah* along with the price of salt herring. Yet, in 1902, in this supposed centre of unworldliness, self-denial and spirituality, far and away the most successful businesswoman in the town was Szabina Almási, the proprietor of the municipality's thriving brothel.

In 1902, Szabina Almási paid 300 *korona* in income tax, an enormous sum in those days.[9] By way of comparison, in the timber trade, one of the most lucrative businesses in Sighet, only a partnership formed by two timber merchants, Glasner and Schüller, paid more taxes.[10] None of the town's lawyers or doctors earned nearly as much as the brothel keeper. At the turn of the twentieth century sex, like timber, was a valuable commodity.

It was rumoured that many of the customers of Sighet's brothel were Ultra-Orthodox Jews and that some of the girls who worked there were also Jewish. One of the girls was reputed to have been well versed in the finer points of the *Talmud* (perhaps she was a rabbi's wayward daughter?) and is said to have enjoyed theological discussions with some of her clients, presumably after she had satisfied their earthly cravings.[11]

Like most progressive-minded Jews living in Budapest and in western Hungary, Adolf and Teréz would have shuddered at the thought of these kaftan-clad Jews, with their unkempt beards and dirty fingernails. Adolf and Teréz had no wish to live in a self-imposed ghetto. As for their son Miklós — my grandfather — he never bothered to disguise his total lack of interest in religion. Miklós seems to have regarded Judaism, or indeed any religion, as little more than a tiresome set of prescriptions grounded in fear, superstition and ignorance.

These days — and for reasons that I'm sure I don't need to elaborate — Jewish parents rarely, if ever, name a child Adolf. But back then, in the latter half of the nineteenth century, German chosen names like Adolf, Gustav and Franz were popular amongst secular-minded Jews in Austria-Hungary. All across the Dual Kingdom, liberal-thinking Jews gave their children German or Hungarian chosen names to show how modern and patriotic they were. In the Hungarian sector of the Empire, many Jews abandoned old-fashioned Hebrew names like Mózes and Ábrahám in favour of popular Hungarian names such as Móritz and Miklós. Only kaftan-wearing *Haredim*, swaying over their prayer books in remote *shtetls* and in towns such as Munkács, Szatmárnémeti and Máramarossziget (Sighet), kept to the old names and the old ways.

When Adolf married Teréz in August 1895, he was twenty-two years old and already living in Budapest. His bride, who was born in the Hungarian capital, was nearly two years younger. From their wedding certificate I know that the fathers of both bride and groom were deceased when the marriage took place and that they had almost certainly been men of modest means. Teréz's father, Ervin, had been a *cipész* or cobbler, plying his trade in Budapest. Adolf's father, Mika, had been an *üveges* or glazier, in the little northern town of Rózsahegy. The wedding certificate also bears the signatures of two witnesses. One, Lipót Fränkl, who may have been a brother or uncle of the groom, gave his occupation as *metsző* or tailor's cutter. The other, József Welmann, is listed as a *szobatisztító* or house-cleaner.

Though a tiny elite of Jewish bankers, financiers and industrialists owned elegant town houses and magnificent country estates, spending their leisure hours with their mistresses, collecting exclusive works of art, and hobnobbing with aristocrats, the overwhelming majority of Austria-Hungary's Jews earned a modest living as petty traders, artisans, or skilled workers. In Budapest, upper working-class Jews like my great-grandparents generally lived in cramped, one-room flats. Frequently, middle-class apartments in Hungary's capital weren't much bigger, consisting of a living room, a bedroom, and a kitchen.

Although Jews like my great-grandparents were better off than factory hands, *napszámos* or day labourers, and many peasants, their lives were still precarious enough. Prolonged illness could bring financial ruin, while competition, especially amongst tradesmen and artisans, was frequently fierce. If my great-grandfather, Adolf Fränkl, dreamed of going into business and of making a better life for himself, he would have been keenly aware of just how easy it was to slip back into abject poverty. At the end of the nineteenth century there were still plenty of Jews in Austria-Hungary, both men and women, who eked out a meagre existence as *napszámos*. Many working-class women, Jews and non-Jews alike, were glad to take jobs as household maids despite low wages, long hours and, not infrequently, the threat of sexual harassment.[12]

Rózsahegy, where my great-grandfather spent his childhood and teenage years, was part of Hungary until the peace settlement following World War One. Then, without moving an inch, the little town, now known as Ružomberok, found itself in Czechoslovakia, along with a substantial tranche of northern Hungary.

I can picture Adolf sighing and shaking his head in disbelief as he heard about these developments. Like most progressive-minded Jews living in what had been the Hungarian portion of the Dual Monarchy, Adolf was a staunch Hungarian patriot. During Hungary's bloody revolt against Austrian rule, which erupted in 1848, a higher proportion of Jews than gentiles had enlisted in the Hungarian defence force, the *Honvéd*.[13] Plenty of Jews had been willing to fight and, if necessary, to die for the Hungarian national cause, which they adopted as their own. Had it not been for the intervention of the Russian Tsar, the Hungarians would almost certainly have triumphed, freeing themselves once and for all from the Austrian yoke. Hungarian *Honvéd* troops, fired up by an irresistible cocktail of patriotism and *pálinka*, trounced Habsburg forces time and again.

For Adolf, as for other Jews weary of exclusion and rejection, Hungary offered the tantalising prospect of belonging.[14] While Jews could rarely, if ever, hope to be fully accepted by Romanians, Russians, Ukrainians, or Slovaks, by the middle of the nineteenth century Hungary's leading element, its nobility, was keen to embrace them. Much like members of other minorities living in the country — Germans, Slovaks, Romanians, Ruthenians etc — Jews were encouraged to reinvent themselves as Hungarians by adopting the Hungarian language as their mother tongue, adapting to Hungarian culture and identifying whole-heartedly with the Hungarian nation.[15]

Take the poet Sándor Petőfi, the very embodiment of romantic nineteenth-century Hungarian nationalism.

Petőfi, who was revered during his lifetime as Hungary's national poet, was the son of a Slovak butcher. Until the poet changed his surname to 'Petőfi', the future embodiment of Hungarian nationalism bore the decidedly un-Hungarian name of 'Petrovics'. As for Petőfi's mother, it was common knowledge that she could barely speak a word of Hungarian. But none of that mattered. It was Petőfi's unwavering commitment to the Hungarian national cause and his effortlessly lyrical command of the Hungarian language that won the admiration and acceptance of his fellow Hungarians.

Peter Lorre

Rózsahegy, where my great-grandfather Adolf spent his childhood, was a backwater. Peter Lorre, the diminutive Hollywood actor who had important supporting roles in such classic American movies as *The Maltese Falcon* and *Casablanca*, is almost certainly the most famous person ever to have come from the town that is now more commonly known by its Slovak name of Ružomberok. Strangely, though, there's no mention of Lorre on the town's otherwise detailed website. Perhaps local historians don't consider Lorre, whose original name was László Löwenstein, to be a true son of Ružomberok? Yet Lorre was born in the town and lived there until his family moved to Brăila, in present-day Romania, when he was five.

Before fleeing to America following the rise of Hitler, Lorre became a highly acclaimed actor in Germany, collaborating with the likes of Bertolt Brecht and Fritz Lang in Berlin and starring in Lang's influential thriller *M*. Lorre's pronounced European accent meant that, although he found work in Hollywood, he was forever typecast as a foreigner. An outsider even in the Rózsahegy of his childhood because he spoke German and Hungarian rather than Slovak, and because his family was Jewish, Lorre ended his days amidst the comforts of California, a professional as well as a literal foreigner.

My great-grandfather, Adolf Fränkl, left Rózsahegy for the Hungarian capital at least a decade before Peter Lorre was born. However, in a small town like Rózsahegy it's inconceivable that the few Jewish families living there wouldn't have known one another. The Löwensteins were a great deal more prosperous and considerably more cultivated than my relatives. Lorre's father, Alajos Löwenstein, a reserve officer in the Austro-Hungarian army, was the chief bookkeeper at a textile mill in Rózsahegy.[16] Fluent in both German and Hungarian, Alajos Löwenstein had studied for three years at a commercial academy, graduating with honours. By contrast, my great-great-grandfather Mika Fränkl, who was living in Rózsahegy during the nine or ten years that Alajos spent there, was a simple, uneducated glazier.

Despite the social and economic disparities between the two families, the Löwensteins and the Fränkls would have been on nodding terms, if nothing else. Whenever a window needed replacing in the Löwenstein household, Alajos Löwenstein, or perhaps his wife, would almost certainly have summoned Mika, my great-great-grandfather, to carry out the work. There would have been ties, however faint and circumscribed, between the two Jewish households.

We know from his wedding certificate that my great-grandfather, Adolf, had left Rózsahegy and was working as a typesetter in Budapest when he married Teréz at the age of twenty-two. For someone as energetic and enterprising as my great-grandfather, Rózsahegy offered limited prospects. To the north of the little town lay the Austrian province of Galicia, with its land-hungry peasants subsisting on tiny plots of land and its teeming population of Poles, Ukrainians and Jews clamouring for emigration. Further north still, beyond the Austro-Hungarian towns of Cracow, Lemberg and Tarnopol (now the Polish city of Craków and the Ukrainian cities of Lviv and Ternopil), loomed the squalor, political upheavals and bloody pogroms of late imperial Russia. Rózsahegy was no place for an ambitious young man, particularly a Jew, to make his mark.

When Adolf left home to embark on a new life in the Hungarian capital, Budapest considered itself the equal of Vienna. In the space of barely fifty years the city, created out of three separate towns — Buda, Óbuda and Pest — had grown into a bustling metropolis with a population almost a million strong. Between 1867 and 1914, Budapest overtook Berlin as the fastest-growing city in Europe.[17] Bridges were thrown across the Danube linking picturesque Buda with sprawling, commercial Pest. Vying with one another in ostentation and splendour, theatres, concert halls, railway stations, apartment buildings, churches and banks were erected in a frenzy of activity. On the shores of the Danube, overlooking the Buda hills, the world's largest parliament building was completed in 1902, incorporating eighty-four pounds of gold leaf. Budapest was a city on the move.

Industries sprang up making everything from munitions to locomotives, from petrol-driven taxis to the world's first electric railway engines.[18] Attracted by the dynamism and wealth of this mercurial city, tens of thousands of peasants and landless agricultural labourers left their villages for the capital, finding work in factories, on building sites or as domestic servants for the burgeoning middle classes. Writers, artists, musicians, actors, architects, engineers and artisans were drawn to Budapest from the provinces, eager to seize the opportunities that only the capital could bestow. And so my great-grandfather Adolf Fränkl, in whom ambition, optimism and energy were only matched by an unerring propensity for failure, came too.

4

How my great-grandfather Adolf decided that two family names are better than one

My great-grandfather Adolf Fränkl qualified as a typesetter in the age of the printed word. When Adolf settled in Budapest in the final decade of the nineteenth century, the city's inhabitants devoured newspapers and periodicals with almost as much relish as *túrós csusza* and roast goose. In an era of growing literacy, and several decades before the introduction of commercial radio, let alone television, the printed word represented an unrivalled source of entertainment, as well as information, for the public at large.

Printing works in Hungary, 1918

Across Hungary the number of newspapers, magazines and journals was multiplying at a dizzying rate. In 1881, 504 different newspapers and journals were published in the country.[19] By the eve of World War One, that figure had spiralled to almost 2,000, while the total number of printed copies rose from 13 million in 1867 to 250 million in 1914. At the turn of the twentieth century, in Budapest alone, there were 22 daily newspapers vying for the reading public's attention.[20]

There was an insatiable demand amongst Hungary's avid population of newspaper readers for accounts of sensational criminal trials, for reviews of the latest exhibitions, concerts, theatrical productions and books, for short stories by the country's most talented and prolific writers, as well as for mundane but nevertheless important information such as the times of trains and the fluctuating prices of grain and livestock.

Newspapers were also the nation's primary source of information about politics. Speeches in the upper and lower houses of Hungary's parliament, the aspirations of the country's small but indefatigable band of feminists, demands by the Dual Monarchy's national minorities for cultural autonomy and equal rights, problems stemming from the influx of impoverished and frequently illiterate Jewish migrants from Galicia, as well as news of major political developments beyond the borders of Austria-Hungary, were all discussed at length. The opportunities for typesetters such as my great-grandfather, as well as for journalists and writers, had never been better.

Typesetters and others involved in the printing process were the unseen technicians without whom editors, journalists and authors wouldn't have been able to reach their burgeoning readership. As aspiring and established writers sipped coffee, beer, wine, or *pálinka* at their accustomed tables in some of Budapest's renowned coffee houses, men like my great-grandfather were toiling away to the mechanical accompaniment of overheated printing presses. Instead of the bewitching aroma of fresh-roasted coffee, cigars, scrambled eggs, beef broth and *eau de cologne*, which would have greeted the nostrils of patrons of the coffee houses, my great-grandfather was accustomed to the more pungent smells of machine oil and printer's ink.

Although typesetters and writers lived in a state of mutual dependence, they inhabited different worlds. It's hard to imagine that, at the end of the working day, after he had taken off his overalls and scrubbed his fingernails, my great-grandfather would have headed for one of the city's elegant coffee houses to meet his friends and to relax over a couple of drinks. It's conceivable that, on his way home, Adolf stopped off for a hurried *stampedli* at one of the city's innumerable, smoke-filled basement taverns. However, it's much more likely that he hurried home to his wife and children. First and foremost, Adolf was a family man who cherished the dream of leaving paid employment and of going into business on his own account. Squandering money in bars and cafés would have been contrary to my great-grandfather's frugal instincts.

Even though Adolf devoted much of his working life to the printed word, I know nothing of his reading habits. My mother says that Miklós, her father — Adolf's eldest son and the most highly educated of his five children — wasn't much of a reader. My mother rarely saw Miklós with a newspaper, let alone a book, in his hands. So, it's quite likely that his parents, Adolf and Teréz, weren't avid readers either.

Even though Adolf and Teréz may have taken little personal interest in Hungary's vibrant literary life, they would almost certainly have heard of some of the era's most popular and talented writers, including Gyula Krúdy who settled in Budapest in 1896, just a few years after my great-grandfather moved to the capital. Aside from their provincial roots and the fact that they both spent much of their adult lives in Budapest, Krúdy and my great-grandfather might seem to have had little in common. Krúdy, whose father had been a successful lawyer and a member of the gentry class, pursued a life of unbridled self-indulgence. Unable to endure the incessant demands and intrusions of conventional family life, Krúdy lived apart from his wives and children, often in hotel rooms, devoting himself to his writing and to an endless succession of amorous conquests.

At one point, Krúdy even managed to shock his current mistress, embarking on a torrid love affair with her sixteen-year-old daughter. Although Krúdy eventually married the young woman and fathered a child with her, he spent hardly any time with his new family. Instead, Krúdy threw himself into fresh romances and frequented the taverns, coffee houses and other places of entertainment that he adored.

Unlike the wayward, sybaritic Krúdy, Adolf Fränkl was a conventional and devoted family man. After marrying Teréz Mandel, in 1895, Adolf appears to have lived contentedly with his wife until Teréz's death from cancer more than forty years later. After her death, Adolf did not remarry, living alone in a rented room in Budapest until his death at the age of sixty-nine in July, 1942.

Yet despite the many and obvious differences between Krúdy and Adolf, there were a number of things that united them. Krúdy, whose first wife was a rabbi's daughter, despised anti-Semitism. In the early 1930s, as Hungary's Jews found themselves increasingly targeted by radical right-wing elements who blamed Jews for all the supposed ills of Hungarian society, Krúdy wrote a series of articles about the notorious Tiszaeszlár affair to remind his readers of the stupidity and viciousness of anti-Semitism. As Krúdy recounted in these articles, which appeared in a daily newspaper, the disappearance of a fourteen-year-old servant girl, Eszter Solymosi, from the village of Tiszaeszlár, in the late nineteenth century, prompted the arrest of several Jewish men who were accused of involvement in her ritual

murder.[21] Despite the lack of *any* credible evidence that a
crime had been committed — and although the young girl's
body was never found — the defendants were held in jail
for fifteen months and tortured in a fruitless effort to make
them confess. The eventual acquittal of the defendants
on all charges provoked outrage and anti-Semitic riots
in Budapest and other towns. Many of Krúdy's fellow
countrymen, including lawyers and other highly educated
elements, found it entirely plausible that Jews would choose
to spend their leisure hours abducting Christian children
in order to drain their blood for use in diabolical religious
rites.

*Adolf Fränkl's wedding certificate,
with the names and dates of birth
of his children*

Aside from being a faithful husband — and there are no
family legends to suggest that Adolf was flirtatious let
alone that he indulged in extra-marital affairs — my great-
grandfather seems to have taken considerable pride in his
children. Adolf painstakingly recorded the given names
and birth dates of each of his five children, in immaculate
copperplate, on the back of his wedding certificate. Miklós,
my grandfather, born on 18 July 1896, was the eldest; Klára,

born on 23 March 1908, was the youngest. Above the children's names, in much smaller letters, my great-grandfather has written *házasságunkból született gyermekek* — 'children arising from our marriage'.

Adolf's choice of a comparatively small font when referring to himself and to his wife — 'arising from our marriage' — as contrasted with his use of a much larger font to record the names and dates of birth of his children — is not without significance. It suggests a personality marked by the absence of ego; a man who could be counted on to put his children first.

However, for someone supposedly family oriented, my great-grandfather made at least one strange and unfathomable decision. In 1911, Adolf applied to change his German-Jewish family name, Fränkl, to the Hungarian 'Faragó'. At the time, many of the country's Germans and Jews were adopting Hungarian family names, whether from pragmatism — a Hungarian surname could be helpful in obtaining employment, particularly in the civil service or in the *Honvéd*'s officer corps — or simply as an expression of their patriotism.[22] But it's puzzling that Adolf should have requested a change of name solely for himself and his eldest son, Miklós, who was fourteen years old at the time.[23] For whatever reason, Adolf saw fit to leave his four younger children with his previous family name, Fränkl. From June 1911, when Adolf was notified that his application had been approved by the Minister of the Interior, Ilona, Jenő, Márton, and Klára, ranging in age from three to twelve, ceased to share a family name with either their father or eldest brother.

When I recorded a series of interviews with my uncle at his home in Toronto in the late 1990s, during a hot Canadian summer, he suggested that his grandfather, Adolf, may have requested a change of name solely for himself and for Miklós because he lacked copies of the birth certificates of his other children, possibly because they had been born outside Budapest. Without the relevant documentation, Bertalan speculated, the authorities wouldn't have approved an alteration in the surnames of his younger children.

However, this narrative of bureaucratic impediments or of bungling or absent-mindedness on the part of my great-grandfather is unconvincing. Whether Adolf's children were born in Budapest or in the provinces, my great-grand-father would have been legally bound to register their births with the civil authorities. Aside from itinerant bands of Gypsies who roamed across the country with their horses and carts and the desperate, mostly unmarried mothers of foundlings, the practice of registering new births was well established in Austria-Hungary by this period. Even if Adolf had somehow failed to obtain copies of the birth certificates of his four younger children when registering them — or if the certificates had been destroyed in a fire or lost in the course of moving from one set of lodgings to another — my great-grandfather could have readily obtained copies of the documents with a little time and trouble.

I will never know for certain why Adolf decided that two family names were better than one. However, his decision was to have far-reaching, if unintended, consequences. In separate conversations, both my mother and uncle empha-sised that Adolf's younger children had felt an enduring sense of rejection, even betrayal, by their father. The fact that Adolf had singled out his eldest son, Miklós, for special treatment only aggravated the other siblings' sense of grievance. Once he was an adult and free to choose his own surname, Miklós' youngest brother, Márton, the most ambitious and successful of Adolf's children, assumed the surname Füredi. The middle brother, Jenő, became Fenyvesi. Like Faragó, both Füredi and Fenyvesi are typical

Hungarian family names, betraying no hint of the brothers' Jewish origins.

Miklós Faragó's school leaving certificate, dated 16 June, 1913

As I write these words, I have my grandfather's school leaving certificate in front of me. Both my mother and uncle are quite certain that Miklós was the only one of Adolf's five children to obtain his *érettségi*. Like their father, Adolf's children were of a practical cast of mind. None of them, not even Miklós, gave any indication of having scholarly leanings.

According to the certificate, Miklós completed his secondary education at the Higher Commercial School in Budapest's Ninth District, little more than a year before the outbreak of World War One. Higher commercial schools were intended to prepare earnest but not particularly gifted young men and women for careers as clerks in insurance companies, banks, and commercial institutions, unlike Hungary's formidably academic gymnasiums, which produced some of the most outstanding mathematicians and theoretical physicists of the twentieth century, including Edward Teller, John von Neumann, and Leó Szilárd.[24]

Despite its comparatively modest status, the higher commercial school that Miklós attended boasted some surprisingly distinguished former teachers and alumnae. Milán Füst, one of Hungary's most highly lauded poets and prose writers of the twentieth century, once taught there, as did the compiler of the first Turkish-Hungarian dictionary, János Pastinszky, and the philosopher Béla Zalai, a friend of the influential Marxist philosopher György Lukács.[25]

Aside from occasional translations into mainstream European languages, the verses of Milán Füst remain virtually unknown outside Hungary. However, Sir Alexander Korda, a former pupil at the Ninth District's Higher Commercial School and a near contemporary of my grandfather, will be familiar to readers in the English-speaking world, particularly film enthusiasts. Then known by his given name, Sándor László Kellner, the future Anglo-American filmmaker left Hungary in 1919, adopting the un-English — but reassuringly non-Jewish — name of 'Korda'.

Unlike my grandfather, who fought for Austria-Hungary in World War One, sustaining serious injuries from which he never fully recovered, Korda was excused military service due to poor eyesight. However, if Korda escaped the horrors of the Great War he could not escape arrest and detention, along with thousands of other suspected Communists, in 1919, following the collapse of the short-lived Hungarian Soviet Republic.[26] After his release from prison, Korda immediately left Hungary, never to return. By contrast, Miklós, in whom a stubborn optimism was allied to an almost total lack of political foresight, never even considered emigrating. My grandfather's ambitions remained characteristically modest and conventional — to recover from his injuries as far as possible, to find work of some kind, whether in Budapest or in the provinces and, in due course, to start a family.

Miklós' *érettségi* makes it abundantly clear that he was a diligent and capable student. Apart from history, in which he was found to be merely 'satisfactory', Miklós was judged to be 'good' or 'outstanding' in every subject he took, including bookkeeping, 'commercial geography', Hungarian language and literature, and 'commercial correspondence' in three languages: Hungarian, German, and French.

Aside from noting his final grades, my grandfather's *érettségi* records his place and date of birth as well as his religion, which is given as 'Israelite'. In reality, neither Miklós nor his parents took much interest in religion or in their Jewish roots. In June 1911, according to the letter informing Miklós' father, Adolf, that his application to change his surname to Faragó had been approved, the family was living in a modest, one-room apartment at 5-7, Kruspér *utca* in Budapest. A short distance from the Technical University, Kruspér *utca* is located in Buda, far from such districts as Terézváros and Erzsébetváros, across the river in Pest, where Jews had settled in large numbers since the mid-nineteenth century. In 1910, approximately ninety-three percent of the city's Jews lived in Pest. It's hard to avoid the conclusion that, in selecting lodgings in a part of Budapest where there were comparatively few Jews, my great-grandfather revealed his indifference to his ancestral religion and to the very notion of leading a 'Jewish life'.

My mother and uncle are in agreement that, after obtaining his *érettségi* in June 1913, Miklós found employment as a clerk with an insurance company in Budapest. Unlike his youngest brother, Jenő, who had struggled at school and who eventually qualified as a typesetter, Miklós wore a suit and tie to work; he spent his days in an office where his knowledge of languages, economics, and geography stood him in good stead.

But my grandfather's lower middle-class idyll was to prove short-lived. Following the assassination of the heir to the Habsburg throne by Serbian nationalists in Sarajevo, in June 1914, Austria-Hungary declared war on Serbia. No one guessed, least of all my grandfather, that the murder of Archduke Franz Ferdinand would prove the catalyst for a war of unprecedented scale and destructiveness.

Miklós, who was eighteen years old at the outbreak of the Great War, was conscripted into Austria-Hungary's over-stretched and hopelessly ill-matched armed forces. The Empire's polyglot troops, including Bosnian infantrymen with their distinctive red fez hats, Hungarian Hussars with their sabres and fur-trimmed capes, and Polish *Uhlan* cavalry armed with carbines and lances, faced a range of implacable foes, including Serbia, Italy, and imperial Russia.

'The Austro-Hungarian army was small, badly-armed, badly led', observed the historian Norman Stone, while the loyalty of many of its Slav conscripts was open to doubt, especially in any future clash with Russia.[27] Crucially, Austria-Hungary had not kept up with her main adversary, Russia, in equipping her forces with modern armaments:[28]

a large part of [Austria-Hungary's] artillery was old-fashioned. The army against Russia had less than 2,000 guns to the Russians' 3,000; even so, there were forty-five different types of gun, each needing different munitions; and a further problem was that many guns were made of bronze which, though much less efficient than steel, lasted longer and therefore suited the exiguous pre-war army budgets.

Yet few Austrians or Hungarians seemed to be aware of these grave deficiencies. News of the declaration of war against Serbia was received with widespread enthusiasm. József Erdélyi, then a high school pupil in Mezőtúr, a small town almost ninety miles southeast of Budapest, recalled that he and his classmates poured onto the streets, yelling at the top of their voices: 'Hurrah for War! Down with Serbia! Down with the Tsar! Long live the King! Long live Emperor Wilhelm II! Hurrah for the [Turkish] *Padishah!*'[29] Across Hungary, Gypsy musicians gathered at railway stations to play for troops heading for the front.

Most of Austria-Hungary's senior politicians and military commanders were supremely confident, particularly as the Empire was allied with Germany.[30] Hardly anyone seems to have considered the possibility that there might not be an early and decisive victory over Serbia, let alone that the Empire could find itself in grave and possibly mortal danger.

Hungarian officers, 1913

5

A good war

In *Magyar Hősök* (*Hungarian Heroes*), a lavishly illustrated book published in Budapest at the height of World War One, readers are presented with hundreds of apparently *bona fide* reports of astonishing acts of heroism and ingenuity by Hungarian soldiers and civilians. To read these stirring accounts and to gaze at the richly coloured illustrations of mounted hussars putting the enemy to flight is to believe in the invincibility as well as the inherent justness of the Hungarian cause. *Magyar Hősök*, which was published in late 1916, was clearly intended to bolster readers' flagging confidence in an eventual victory by Austria-Hungary and its allies, as well as their capacity for further exertion and self-sacrifice.

Lajos Platschek (left) with
his brother Dezső

Take the story of eighty-two-year-old Márton Kerekes, a grizzled veteran of the 1848 Hungarian revolt against Habsburg rule. Kerekes and his neighbours, smallholders in the rugged hill country north of Sighet, received news that a force of Russian troops had been sighted on Hungarian soil, heading directly towards their village. Declining to take flight or to wait passively at home for the Russians to arrive, Kerekes immediately set about organising armed resistance.[31] Rallying a hundred and eighty men from the immediate locality, who armed themselves with scythes, hoes and other agricultural implements, Kerekes, dressed in his antique uniform and brandishing a sabre, placed himself at the head of this motley force and set off to confront the enemy. Along the way, the band was augmented by five gendarmes, armed with rifles, and two excise men.

Of course, it could be objected that Kerekes, far from being a hero and a patriot, was simply a meddlesome old fool, a Carpathian Don Quixote. After all, Kerekes had hectored his under-equipped neighbours into joining an enterprise that would almost certainly result in their deaths without securing any obvious military advantage. Scythes and hoes are no match for breach-loading rifles and machine guns.

Although the veteran Kerekes and a significant part of his rag-tag force met their deaths in the eventual encounter with the invading Russian troops, they managed to hold off the Russians for three hours, which was no mean feat. According to the account in *Magyar Hősök*, Kerekes' men set fire to a bridge spanning a small river, which the Russians would have to cross in order to continue their advance. With no option but to enter the water, the Russian troops were pelted with stones as they waded across the river and slashed with scythes and other agricultural implements as they tried to scramble up the bank on the opposite side, where Kerekes and his peasant militia was deployed. While the eventual outcome of this starkly unequal combat was never in any doubt, and although Hungarian fatalities were alarmingly high, the ferocious resistance put up by Kerekes and his band of patriotic smallholders was remarkable.

Or consider the account of the valorous conduct of Corporal Mandel Katz who, in civilian life, was a trader in a small town in present-day Slovakia. This story merits attention for a number of reasons. In the first place, Corporal Katz displayed exceptional bravery, tactical sense and leadership skills, as well as ruthlessness. With just forty-three Hungarian infantrymen under his command, Katz mounted a successful attack on an enemy force comprising four thousand Russian troops![32]

According to *Magyar Hősök*, the infantry unit commanded by Corporal Katz managed to cross enemy lines unobserved, in dense fog, catching a group of Russian officers off guard. The officers, who had been warming themselves by a fire, were cut down in a sudden hail of bullets, leaving one lieutenant colonel, one captain, two first lieutenants, one lieutenant, one adjutant, several non-commissioned officers, and twelve rank and file soldiers lying dead. An additional forty Russian troops raised their arms and surrendered to Katz and his men, while the remainder of the substantial Russian force, unaware of their overwhelming numerical superiority, simply fled.

Aside from the startling nature of Corporal Katz's victory over a much larger body of enemy troops, the published account of his military exploits is noteworthy because, as Mandel Katz's name clearly suggests, he was a Jew. At the time, neither the editors of *Hungarian Heroes* nor Mandel Katz saw any contradiction between being a Jew *and* a loyal Hungarian. In a national census conducted in 1900, no less than seventy-two per cent of Hungary's Jews stated that they considered themselves Hungarian in terms of their cultural and political identity.[33]

For Mandel Katz, as for Hungary's wartime prime minister, István Tisza, a man's religion was a private matter. Loyal and valorous Hungarians were to be found amongst all of the major religious denominations in Hungary, not least Jews. During World War One, the country's sizeable and comparatively well-educated Jewish population provided approximately 300,000 soldiers for Austria-Hungary's armies.[34] These included 25,000 officers and no fewer than 25 generals. In addition, thousands of skilled Jewish professionals, in such vital fields as medicine, pharmacology, dentistry, engineering, and veterinary science, made a significant contribution to Austria-Hungary's war effort. While precise data is unavailable, it's clear that tens of thousands of Hungarian Jews were killed in action and many more, including Miklós, my maternal grandfather, suffered life-changing injuries.

Yet the economic, social and other tensions in Hungarian society, that became increasingly unmanageable as the War dragged on, were eagerly exploited by opposition politicians and by much of the Catholic press, resulting in widespread accusations that Jews were profiteers, cowards and fundamentally unassimilable.[35] The process of scapegoating and vilifying Hungary's Jews only intensified after Austria-Hungary's defeat in World War One and in the wake of the humiliating peace treaty imposed on Hungary by the Allied Powers. By late summer 1941, with the radical right in the ascendancy across much of Europe, the idea that a Jew could be entrusted with weapons and permitted to serve in Hungary's armed forces had become anathema. If Mandel Katz had been of military age in late 1941, he would have been conscripted into an auxiliary labour battalion along with some of the country's finest doctors, scholars, poets, musicians, and artists. Katz might have found himself digging anti-tank ditches or unloading goods wagons in sub-zero temperatures, without warm clothing, decent shelter, proper food, or medical care. Like some of the Jews conscripted into the labour battalions, Mandel Katz might have been ordered, at gunpoint, to walk across a minefield to detonate unexploded mines. Or he could have been sent up a tree and used for target-practice by the battalion's non-commissioned officers. One thing is quite certain: Mandel Katz's formidable military skills wouldn't have been called upon.

By the eve of World War Two, following the passage of sweeping Anti-Jewish Laws — and after years of unrelenting anti-Semitic invective from many of Hungary's leading clerics, politicians, and intellectuals — Mandel Katz would have been treated as a pariah by most of his fellow countrymen. Even if he had converted to Christianity, become a devout Catholic priest, declared himself an atheist, married a Hungarian noblewoman (before the interdiction of marriages between Jews and gentiles, naturally), captured a notorious enemy agent, or invented a weapon of mass destruction for the sole use of the Hungarian army, Mandel Katz wouldn't have been able to redeem himself. If he had walked on water or performed a host of other tricks, involving loaves and fishes, Mandel Katz would still have been labelled a Jew, with scant prospect of escaping his fate.

After the War, scarcely anyone in Hungary remembered the heroic exploits of Mandel Katz. The valour and patriotism displayed by Katz and celebrated in *Magyar Hősök* quickly faded into oblivion. On the other hand, almost every literate Hungarian would have been aware of the *fictional* Jews portrayed in an influential novel published in 1919, *The Village That Was Swept Away*.

While Mandel Katz was risking his life fighting the enemies of Austria-Hungary, and while my great-uncle Ágoston and grandfather Miklós struggled to hold back the Italian forces that threatened to overrun a large swathe of the Empire — depriving Austria-Hungary of its only stretch of coastline — Dezső Szabó was scribbling away in his cosy schoolmaster's study in Lőcse (now Levoča in present-day Slovakia), putting the finishing touches to the manuscript of *The Village That Was Swept Away* (*Az Elsodort Falu*).

Dezső Szabó

Szabó's novel was completed in August 1918, just a few months before the end of the War. Published in the summer of the following year, *The Village That Was Swept Away* proved an enormous and unexpected success. It rapidly established itself as one of the most popular and influential works of fiction to appear in Hungary in the inter-war era. According to the literary critic Béla Pomogáts, the book's central ideas had an immediate and major influence on literary and political life in the country, 'determining the path of entire generations in the decades after its publication'.[36]

Szabó's beliefs, which he succeeded in implanting in many of his readers' minds, were reactionary and xenophobic. The novel extolled the virtues of traditional Hungarian village life, while deploring the influence of the country's Germans and Jews on Hungarian society. Szabó identified Germans and Jews, in particular, with the dissemination of such modern 'evils' as socialism, capitalism, liberalism, and democracy.

The Village That Was Swept Away presented readers with a succession of anti-Semitic stereotypes. In place of the valorous and authentic Mandel Katz — and of the tens of thousands of patriotic Jews who had fought for Austria-Hungary — Szabó served up a number of crudely racist fictional caricatures, including a cowardly Jewish bank clerk. Summoned to appear at a provincial recruiting station, where his fitness to serve in the Empire's armed forces was to be assessed by doctors, the bank clerk was deceitful and cowardly:[37]

A tall, scrawny Jewish youth came forward hesitantly. He was tottering in such a way that, with every step, it seemed he would collapse… He had prepared for the medical assessment as if it were a difficult exam. For weeks he had eaten less and less each day until he had grown thin… he had stayed up each night and he had drunk so much strong black coffee that the ticking of his heart sounded like someone striking a bell. By masturbating repeatedly, he had succeeded in producing an inflamed swelling on his groin, which allowed him to complain of a hernia. He had sprayed some sort of liquid into his eyes, so that they were sore and swollen… All through the nights he had practised coughing in a hollow, deathly fashion. And every night he tightly bound his legs in two places so that the veins would appear black and swollen…

The literary merits of *The Village That Was Swept Away* have been hotly disputed. Dezső Kosztolányi, one of the most gifted writers to emerge in Hungary in the first half of the twentieth century, mocked Szabó's novel, declaring that it must be the work of a talentless imposter who had appropriated Szabó's name and reputation in order to increase his otherwise meagre sales. In a review of the book which appeared in the journal *Új Nemzedék* in November 1920, Kosztolányi dismissed *The Village That Was Swept Away* with the damning comment that he could not discern the creative powers of a true novelist anywhere in Szabó's text.[38]

But if the book was a failure in literary terms, it was undoubtedly a commercial and cultural triumph. As the writer and literary critic Antal Szerb ruefully acknowledged, by the 1930s Dezső Szabó had become, 'the preeminent figure in Hungary's intellectual and spiritual life'.[39] For many Hungarians who came of age after the Great War, it was Dezső Szabó's fictional Jews, including the cowardly, dissembling bank clerk, and Gutman, the rapacious, physically repulsive businessman, who defined their understanding of Jews and of the minority's supposedly baleful influence on Hungarian society.

'My father attended the Ludovica,' Zsuzsa tells me with evident pride. 'He was an officer in the army.' During World War One, Zsuzsa's father, Ágoston Weisz, completed an officer training course at the elite Ludovica Military Academy. Occupying a massive neo-classical building in Budapest's Eighth District, the Ludovica was founded in the nineteenth century to train officer cadets for the army as well as to provide instruction for serving army officers.

Ágoston Weisz with his wife, Juliska, and their daughter Zsuzsa

By the end of the century, when it was granted the status of a full military academy, the Ludovica was considered to be on a par with the prestigious Athenaeum in Vienna.

Zsuzsa and I are sitting in her comfortable living room in Wekerletelep, a pretty residential district of Budapest, built in the early decades of the twentieth century. Although she and I are related, we hardly know one another. Zsuzsa's father was the younger of my grandmother Etelka's brothers. For much of the time, particularly after they were adults, Ágoston and Etelka rarely spoke to one another. Each nursed a profound sense of grievance towards the other that notions of kinship or family solidarity were unable to dispel. Alike in that they were intensely proud as well as stubborn, character traits that they had no doubt inherited from their parents, Ágoston and Etelka mostly kept their distance from one another.

As we leaf through a family album, Zsuzsa tells me that her father had been extremely athletic in his youth, with a passion for team sports, particularly football. Several years before World War One, Ágoston was already a member of the youth team of Ferencváros (universally known as 'Fradi' or the FTC), one of Budapest's leading football clubs. In 1913, at the age of just eighteen, he had been appointed manager of the youth team, an unusually onerous responsibility for someone so young.

Ágoston's playing career had been brought to an abrupt end just a few months before the end of the First World War. An infantry officer, he was wounded while serving on the Italian front, sustaining a serious injury to one of his ankles. For the remainder of his life, Ágoston walked with a pronounced limp and wore orthopaedic shoes that were specially made for him.

'My father was wounded in the Italian Alps on 13 June 1918,' Zsuzsa says, with characteristic precision. Speaking in Hungarian, she adds that her father was injured in a battle at the *Tonalei szoros*. The *Passo del Tonale*, as it's known in Italian, is a bleak mountain pass situated south west of the town of Bolzano. During World War One, Italy succeeded in wresting this mountainous terrain from Austria-Hungary, albeit at enormous cost in human lives.

In comparison with the Gallipoli campaign, Passchendaele, or the Battle of the Somme, comparatively little has been written or broadcast in English about the fierce battles between the Italian and Austro-Hungarian armies during World War One. Yet, as the historian Mark Thompson has pointed out, '[s]ome of the most savage fighting of the Great War' took place on this front, with the loss of around a million men who 'died in battle, of wounds and disease or as prisoners.'[40] In contrast to the Second World War, when Italian troops earned a reputation as poor and irresolute soldiers, with no stomach for sustained fighting, in World War One Italian armies often fought tenaciously for the 'recovery' of territory that they considered part of their national patrimony.

If Zsuzsa is correct concerning the date and the place where her father was wounded, then Ágoston must have been injured during a comparatively minor skirmish. Just two days later, on 15 June 1918, a massive Austro-Hungarian offensive commenced further east, along the Piave River. Almost sixty Austro-Hungarian divisions were committed to this campaign, which ended in abject failure and in the loss of 118,000 Austro-Hungarian troops who were killed, injured, captured, or declared missing.[41]

By the time Ágoston was wounded, in June 1918, the armies of Austria-Hungary were in a pitiful state. Troops had to contend with inadequate supplies of weapons and ammunition, worn-out uniforms and boots, and very little food. As Mark Thompson notes in his book *The White War*, a gripping account of the fighting on the Italian front, the daily ration for Austria-Hungary's front-line troops in Italy was reduced to 300 grams of bread and 200 grams of meat in January 1918.[42] In reality, many soldiers no longer received even these meagre rations, forcing them to forage for something to eat. In the early months of 1918, while my great-uncle Ágoston remained at his post, determined to fulfil his duties as an officer in the army of Austria-Hungary, approximately 200,000 Hungarian soldiers deserted, worn down by fatigue, hunger, and mounting concern for their families.

Unlike Ágoston, who thrived in the army, it's hard to imagine that Miklós, my mild-mannered grandfather, was a natural soldier. Miklós lacked Ágoston's martial spirit and natural air of authority, as well as his future brother-in-law's fondness for masculine company. In contrast to Petőfi, the celebrated Hungarian poet who courted death on the battle-field near Segesvár in July 1849, Miklós valued family and personal ties more highly than abstract notions of glory or national destiny. While Petőfi unhesitatingly chose death over life once it had become clear that Hungary's revolt against Habsburg rule was doomed, Miklós would have considered such behaviour foolish.

Yet, my grandfather had a keen and overriding sense of duty. It would never have occurred to him to try to evade conscription, unlike the fictional Jewish bank clerk in *The Village That Was Swept Away*. After receiving his call-up papers, and following a perfunctory medical examination, Miklós was sent for basic training and then assigned to one of the Empire's battered infantry regiments, strung out along barren mountain slopes, facing the Italian forces.

Hungarian soldiers on the Italian front, 1917

There are no surviving photographs of Miklós in army uniform, unlike the photo of my paternal grandfather, Lajos Platschek, and his younger brother, Dezső. In that photograph, which is reproduced at the beginning of this chapter, Dezső appears almost nonchalant, supremely confident that Austria-Hungary and its allies will prevail. Sporting the full dress uniform of a Reserve Second Lieutenant in an infantry regiment, his gloved left hand is resting lightly on his sword. There are three medals pinned on his chest, two of which are for valour in the face of the enemy.[43]

In contrast to his suave, self-assured younger brother, my grandfather Lajos looks uncomfortable, almost sheepish. Although the two brothers are linking arms in a casual display of familial intimacy and male comradeship, it's clear from the photograph that the young men aren't equals. While Dezső is a highly decorated army officer, Lajos's coarsely cut uniform, with a single stripe on the sleeve and a small button in his collar, indicates that he's an enlisted infantryman. Unlike Dezső, it seems that Lajos wasn't viewed as officer material, despite his school leaving certificate and a teaching diploma.

The author of *The Village That Was Swept Away* would have been shocked to learn that Dezső and Lajos were Jews, just like my great-uncle Ágoston Weisz and maternal grandfather Miklós Faragó, both of whom served on the Italian front during the Great War. Proud Hungarians of the Mosaic faith, the men of my family were united in their determination to do their duty, whatever the cost.

Yet even if there are no surviving photographs of Miklós in uniform — and it's possible that none were taken — I have a number of official papers that provide some details of his army service. One of these is a document, dated 12 October 1940, which states that Miklós completed an officer's training course on 15 April 1918 and that he was appointed a *Tartalékos Zászlós*, or Reserve Officer Cadet, on 1 July of that year.

The term *Tartalékos*, or 'Reserve', is misleading. By the spring of 1918, Austria-Hungary had practically no reserve officers to draw upon. After almost four years of fighting, an alarming proportion of the Empire's junior career army officers had been killed, injured, or taken prisoner. New officers like Miklós had to be trained as quickly as possible to take their place. Many of those selected for officer training during the War were high school graduates who had already served in the ranks. They frequently found themselves back on the front line as soon as their accelerated training was completed.

Within weeks of his appointment as a *Tartalékos Zászlós*, Miklós was badly wounded during a fierce artillery barrage. 'For months, he was completely paralysed down his right side,' says my mother. 'He couldn't move his right hand or his right leg and he couldn't speak. He had to learn to write with his left hand.'

Unlike Zsuzsa, who knows the precise circumstances in which her father had been wounded in the First World War, my mother can't tell me very much about when or where Miklós was injured, other than that it happened 'somewhere on the Italian front'. After returning to civilian life, Miklós seems to have made a conscious decision to live entirely in the present and to avoid talking about the War. It's as if my grandfather had placed everything he had seen and experienced as a soldier inside an iron chest that he had sealed and buried deep underground, where its contents could not contaminate him or those whom he loved.

If my mother doesn't know exactly when or where her father was injured, she is adamant that Miklós spent months undergoing treatment in military hospitals and nursing homes before he was judged well enough to be sent to live with his parents. Because of the severity of his injuries, he received a war invalidity pension for the remainder of his life.

'He was terribly lame,' says my mother. 'He used to drag his right foot along the ground.' My mother slowly gets up from the armchair in which she has been sitting and shows me how her father walked. 'He could only walk very slowly,' she adds.

My mother walks slowly too, although that is a consequence of extreme old age. Miklós was barely twenty-two years old when he was wounded in the Great War. He had his whole life ahead of him.

6

The disappearance and presumed death of the Baroness

O n 17 November 1918, less than two weeks after an armistice was concluded between an exhausted Austria-Hungary and the Allies, the robbery and probable murder of Baroness Schönberg was reported in *Máramaros*, a Hungarian-language newspaper published in Sighet. The article informed readers that the Baroness had been travelling to Munkács, now the Ukrainian city of Munkachevo, when her horse-drawn carriage was fired on by unknown assailants.[44] One of the Baroness's horses was killed and her coachman was injured.

Fő tér, Sighet, 1917

An unnamed eyewitness stated that, as the carriage came to a juddering halt, the Baroness had clambered out of the vehicle and started to make her way on foot in the direction of Munkács, leaving the wounded coachman to fend for himself. It was feared that the Baroness, who was thought to be carrying a large quantity of money and valuables, had been robbed and killed.

A week earlier, on 10 November, *Máramaros* had reported that Baroness Schönberg's isolated mansion, near the village of Szolyva, had been ransacked.[45] The windows had been broken and furniture and other household items had been smashed in an orgy of destruction; the Baroness's prized herd of cattle had been driven off. The Baroness, who had been staying at the mansion when it came under attack, had managed to escape unnoticed, finding temporary refuge in Szolyva.

For some months, brazen acts of vandalism and robbery had become increasingly commonplace, particularly in outlying areas of the country such as Máramaros county, where Hungarians were heavily outnumbered by ethnic Ruthenians and Romanians. Although Hungarians (including Jews who identified as Hungarians) constituted a clear majority in towns including Sighet, they accounted for less than fifteen per cent of the population of Máramaros county as a whole.[46]

Around the same time that the drunken mob sacked Baroness Schönberg's handsome mansion, there were other incidents of looting and violence in several villages in the surrounding area. Chaim Rosenthal, a Jewish resident of Kőrösmező (now Yasinya, in the Ukraine) who was most likely an innkeeper or the proprietor of a shop, was shot and killed in this largely Ruthenian-populated village.[47] Rosenthal's wife was seriously wounded in the same incident.

In its issue of 10 November, *Máramaros* reported the arrival in Sighet of a detachment of troops from the 34th Hungarian Infantry Regiment, sent by the authorities in Budapest to quell the recent disturbances. An article in the same paper announced that Sighet's only cinema was to reopen shortly, with shows at six and eight each evening, now that 'public order and peace have been restored and the streets are lit up once more after nightfall'.

But perhaps the most bizarre news item in this issue of *Máramaros* was a lengthy article welcoming the arrival in Sighet of a detachment of 'Zionists'.[48] In November 1918, almost thirty years before the founding of the state of Israel, the term 'Zionist' was a relative novelty, lacking the controversial, frequently pejorative connotations that the word has attracted in certain quarters in recent times.

The Zionists, comprising bold young Jewish-Hungarian men, many of whom had seen active service in the War, arrived late one night by train from Budapest. They belonged to Hungary's small but growing Zionist movement, which was committed to Jewish renewal through the creation of a sovereign Jewish state in Palestine.

The paramilitary Zionist detachment — the paper omitted to mention whether the Zionists wore uniforms or had any identifying insignia — included several young men who had grown up in Sighet and whose families still lived in the town. According to the newspaper, the group's mission was to help protect civilians and civilian property in Sighet and in the surrounding villages. Until the Nazi-orchestrated deportation of Sighet's Jews to Auschwitz, in May 1944, almost 38 per cent of the town's inhabitants had been Jews.[49]

Máramaros reported that, after a formal welcome at Sighet's railway station, with speeches by local dignitaries, the Zionists were conducted to the Hungaria Hotel. Here, in the establishment's splendid restaurant, the men were served tea and cakes by solicitous young ladies from the municipality's Cultural Association of Jewish Young Women. A number of fleeting romances and even a marriage or two may have resulted from this dramatic nocturnal encounter.

While the Zionists were doing their best to protect life and property in Sighet and in the nearby villages — and while the body of Baroness Schönberg lay undiscovered in a roadside ditch somewhere between Szolyva and Munkács — the Austro-Hungarian Empire was slowly falling apart. The Empire that had once seemed so majestic and invincible, both to the imperious Baroness and to my low-born grandfather, simply crumbled away.

In late October 1918, the Czechs declared independence from Austria-Hungary.[50] The Empire's Polish subjects proclaimed their sovereignty in the same month. Soon afterwards, Austria-Hungary's Croats, Slovenes, and Serbs affirmed their allegiance to a separate entity that eventually became Yugoslavia. In mid-November, a newly installed government in Budapest, headed by the radical Leftist Count Gyula Károlyi, declared the establishment of an independent Hungarian Republic.[51] The Old Empire, with its vibrant if sometimes discordant mix of faiths, languages, and nationalities — and its quaintly civilized notions of legality, tolerance, and governmental restraint — passed into history.

Hungary's new premier and his scholarly Minister of Nationality Affairs, Oszkár Jászi, tried hard to appease the country's fractious minorities.[52] But the politicians' well-intentioned efforts had come too late. Several million Slovaks, Romanians, and Serbs, whose homes lay inside Hungary's historic borders, were no longer satisfied with offers of minority rights or even autonomy. They clamoured for self-determination and for the right to decide their own fate. On 1 December, Romanians in Transylvanian Hungary declared their union with the Romanian Kingdom.[53] Around the same time, Hungary's Slovaks affirmed their commitment to inclusion in the new state of Czechoslovakia.

Like wolves stalking a wounded and once dangerous prey, Hungary's neighbours attacked swiftly and without warning. On 17 November 1918, an article in *Máramaros* reported that Serbian and Romanian armies had breached Hungary's frontiers in the south and east. In the north, fighting had erupted with the newly declared state of Czechoslovakia in areas in which ethnic Slovaks heavily outnumbered Hungarians.[54] Exhausted by several years of relentless war and riven by internal dissent, Hungary seemed powerless to resist.

Throughout these anxious and uncertain months, while borders shifted, empires collapsed, and brash new nation states arose in their place, my grandfather, newly discharged from hospital, was recuperating at his parents' home in Balatonfüred, a pretty lakeside spa town some 110 kilometres southwest of Budapest. At some point before the outbreak of World War One, Adolf and Teréz had left Budapest and moved to Balatonfüred, whose waters are reputed to have excellent curative powers, particularly for ailments of the heart. Adolf is said to have established a number of small businesses in Balatonfüred, including a gift shop and a printing works. Here, far from the strife along Hungary's collapsing frontiers, Miklós' days were spent relearning to walk, practising writing with his left hand, and playing *ulti* with neighbours and with other reserve army officers who happened to be living nearby.

With his indifference to history — of all the subjects that my grandfather studied at the commercial high school in Budapest, history was the only one in which his performance was judged merely 'satisfactory' — it's unsurprising that Miklós failed to recognise that an epoch had come to a sudden end. But history has a way of catching you unawares if you don't pay it enough attention. While my grandfather was recuperating in Balatonfüred and pondering the future course of his life, a new phase of history was beginning. Although Miklós didn't realise it at the time, the signs were already there. But then I am looking backwards, my eyes know what to expect. It was much harder for my grandfather; there was no one to guide him or to tell him what to look out for. The 'long nineteenth century', as historians have dubbed it, was over. A century of almost continuously expanding freedom, security, and prosperity in Europe and North America already seemed like a bygone age. Although Miklós didn't know it yet, he was living in modern times.

Part Two

Living in Modern Times

7

Why my grandfather wasn't a Bolshevik even though he was a Jew

In photographs, Cécile Tormay is almost always unsmiling. Born in Budapest in 1875, to titled parents of German descent, Tormay appears prim, aloof, disapproving. Yet, despite her conservative taste in clothes and her reactionary views on politics, Tormay was a revolutionary. In an age when women, particularly upper-class women, were expected to be little more than decorous companions, capable of producing healthy male heirs for their husbands, Tormay chose to remain single and to pursue a career as a writer.

Cécile Tormay

Tormay's first book, a collection of short stories, was published in 1895. Her break-through novel, *Emberek a kövek közt* or *People Among the Rocks*, appeared in 1911. A torrid and far-fetched love story, the novel was translated into several languages, including English, German, Italian, and French.

In Hungary, Tormay is best remembered not as a novelist or as a writer of short stories but as the author of an extraordinary 'diary' covering the period from late October 1918 to the first week of August of the following year. Published in English in two volumes as *An Outlaw's Diary*,[1] with an effusive foreword by the 8th Duke of Northumberland, the book is a vivid and clearly heart-felt account of an exceptionally turbulent period in modern Hungarian history, as recounted by an educated, upper-class Hungarian woman whose social and political instincts were deeply reactionary.

Although written in the form of a diary, many Hungarian scholars have concluded that *An Outlaw's Diary* is largely a work of fiction as well as a none-too-subtle exercise in anti-Semitic propaganda.[2] However, Tormay always insisted that her chronicle, which quickly became a runaway success in Hungary, was 'based' on real facts and events, even if she did not necessarily experience all of them personally.

Much of Tormay's 'diary' bears witness to the ruthless, tyrannical, and radically egalitarian policies pursued by a Communist regime that held power in Hungary for just 133 days in the spring and summer of 1919. Tormay's visceral aversion to Marxist-Leninist ideology, to the disruption of Hungary's age-old social and political order and, not least, to Jews, many of whom occupied prominent positions in the short-lived Communist administration, is palpable.

To her many admirers, Cécile Tormay is a fearless chronicler of the despotism, incompetence, and brutality of the Communists who ruled Hungary for a few months in 1919, less than two years after the outbreak of the Bolshevik revolution in Russia and following a series of left-wing revolts in Germany. However, to her equally numerous detractors, Tormay is a snob, a reactionary, and an incorrigible anti-Semite. In her diary entry for 29 March 1919, she wrote that '[h]umanity has sometimes forgotten the plans and the power of the Jews. The fate of Egypt, the conquest of Canaan, the dissolution of Rome, the religious strife in Byzantium, the decline of Spain… these and many other things.'[3] Or consider this passage from 9 April in the same year:[4]

> The Jew comes uninvited and declines to go when dismissed. He spreads and yet holds together. He penetrates the bodies of the nations. He invisibly organises his own nation among alien peoples. He creates laws beyond the law… He complains of his isolation but builds secret ways as arteries of the boundless city which has by now spread practically throughout the world. His connections and communications reach everywhere… What the Jew finds ridiculous in other people, he keeps fanatically alive in himself. He teaches anarchy and rebellion only to the gentiles, he himself obeys blindly the directions of his invisible leaders.

Despite her impeccable grasp of German, English, Latin, and French, and for all her good taste, erudition, and literary accomplishments, Cécile Tormay was in the grip of a severe and incurable malady. Instead of hobgoblins, *dybbuks*, the Loch Ness Monster, Bigfoot, flying saucers, or little green aliens from remote galaxies, Cécile Tormay believed in an international Jewish conspiracy stretching back thousands of years. Instead of *real* Jews, like my maternal grandfather Miklós, or my great-uncle Ágoston — patriotic, uncompli-cated, ordinary men who fought for Austria-Hungary in the Great War and who often struggled to find work in the peace that followed — Cécile was obsessed with the notion of diabolical *imaginary* Jews, possessing limitless powers, whom she blamed for every human catastrophe beginning with the collapse of the empires of antiquity. Undaunted by the absence of any credible supporting evidence, Cécile had persuaded herself that a cabal of malign and invisible Jewish conspirators — fabulously wealthy, fiendishly clever, and boundlessly ambitious — was surreptitiously encouraging the spread of Marxist revolution *and* global capitalism in order to attain world domination for themselves and their co-religionists.

Cécile had no difficulty in believing that wild-eyed Jewish revolutionaries, with their pistols and leather trench coats, were covertly collaborating with sleek Jewish plutocrats who spent their leisure hours at the racetrack or with their blonde gentile mistresses. Cécile was convinced that all of them, Marxists and capitalists alike, were committed to realising a global Jewish masterplan of unparalleled scope and audacity. Of course, Cécile Tormay's belief in a sinister, worldwide Jewish conspiracy wasn't new. Christians, even educated Christians, had been saying that sort of thing for years.†

Although the idea of a worldwide Jewish masterplan was a gentile-inspired fiction, many right-wing commentators, including Cécile Tormay, saw the triumph of the Hungarian Soviet in 1919 as further proof of the Jews' dastardly intentions. Well over half of the commissars who headed the Hungarian Soviet, as well as significant numbers of mid-level functionaries in the new administration, were of Jewish descent. According to the historian and Hebraist Géza Komoróczy, at least 15 out of 29 members of the

† The notion of an international Jewish conspiracy has drawn much of its inspiration from a notorious tract fabricated in the final decade of the nineteenth century by agents of the *Okhrana*, an arm of the Russian secret service. Purporting to be a blueprint for Jewish global domination, the *Protocols of the Elders of Zion* was an elaborate hoax perpetrated by fiercely anti-Semitic and reactionary Russian elements.

Revolutionary Governing Council established by Hungary's Communists had Jewish origins.[5] These included Béla Kun, the *de facto* leader of the revolutionary government, Jenő Varga, the Commissar for Financial Affairs, and József Pogány, Commissar for Military Affairs. However, as Komoróczy is careful to point out, plenty of non-Jews actively collaborated with the Soviet, including men such as József Cserny, a former naval rating and leather worker, who commanded a terror unit responsible for dozens of deaths.[6]

Far from occupying a privileged position during the months that Hungary's Soviet regime clung to power, as Cécile Tormay claims in her diary, Jews and Jewish institutions featured prominently amongst the Communists' victims. In all, 570 people were sentenced to death by the Revolutionary Tribunal established by the Soviet, of whom 44 were Jews, while an unknown number of Jews were murdered in Hungary's Communist-orchestrated terror.[7] Of 715 'counterrevolutionaries' imprisoned without trial under the Soviet, no fewer than 160 were Jews, including Manfréd Weiss, a prominent industrialist.[8] Weiss, a former member of Hungary's Upper House, was repeatedly tortured while in prison, leading him to attempt suicide.

As early as April 1919, the Hungarian Soviet closed down all Jewish institutions, including the *Chevra Kadisha* or 'bereavement society'.[9] Jewish newspapers and magazines were banned, while the assets of religious institutions, both Jewish and Christian, were confiscated. Jewish and non-Jewish landowners, businessmen, industrialists, and bankers were deprived of their property in sweeping measures of nationalization, while stringent limits were imposed on the number of rooms that a family could occupy.[10] Jewish traders and shopkeepers, like their non-Jewish peers, were frequently branded as 'saboteurs' by the Soviet and blamed for shortages of food and other essentials that gave rise to growing anger and disillusionment amongst the general public. It's hardly surprising that the vast majority of Hungary's Jews loathed Marxism and revolution of any kind.

Apart from considerations of religious faith — Communism's categorical rejection of religion was anathema to the observant — even most secular-minded Jews were deeply suspicious of Marxism and its utopian claims. The great majority of Hungary's Jews — whether shopkeepers, mill owners, artisans, small businessmen, book-keepers, doctors, teachers, bank-clerks, veterinarians, or engineers — were keenly aware that they had far more to lose than to gain from the triumph of Marxism-Leninism and the establishment of the 'dictatorship of the proletariat'.

Far from being committed Bolsheviks, most of Hungary's Jews, including Miklós, Etelka, and other members of my family, were fundamentally conservative, like their non-Jewish peers. The overwhelming majority of Jews aspired to modest, incremental improvements in their working lives and living standards: a larger apartment, better furniture, nicer clothes, a white-collar job or promotion and a higher salary, the possibility of starting up a small business, or of growing an existing one. Only a small minority of Hungary's Jews — some of whom had been introduced to Marxism-Leninism while held as prisoners of war in Russia — dreamt of wholesale revolution, with all of the uncertainties, chaos, and dangers that that entailed. Even Miklós, my grandfather, who had little, if anything, to lose by way of property, income, or professional standing, kept his distance from Béla Kun and the Soviet. I have a sworn affidavit to prove it.

Why my grandfather wasn't a Bolshevik

Affidavit confirming that Miklós Faragó behaved like 'an upstanding Hungarian patriot'

The affidavit, which is dated 15 April 1940, more than twenty years *after* the ousting of the Hungarian Soviet, was drawn up in Balatonfüred. According to my uncle, Miklós' parents Adolf and Teréz had moved to this pretty spa town and lakeside resort sometime before the outbreak of World War One. With far less competition than in the capital and lower start-up costs, Adolf was finally able to realise his long-standing ambition of starting his own business. Miklós, who would have needed help and support long after he was discharged by army physicians, joined his parents in the lakeside town.

The affidavit, which is signed by two reserve army officers — Captain József Fekete and veterinarian Dr. Vilmos Fefer — states that Miklós had played no part in either the establishment or the prolongation of the Hungarian Soviet in 1919:[11]

The undersigned declare upon their honour and with due regard to their professional responsibilities that Miklós Faragó, formerly a Reserve Officer Cadet, whom they knew personally from 1918 to 1922 and with whom they were in constant personal contact between 3 October 1918

89

and 5 August 1919, was not involved in either the prepa-
ration of the revolution or its continuance, and that he
always conducted himself like an upstanding Hungarian
patriot and as befits a reserve officer.

My grandfather's unequivocal rejection of Bolshevism
and of the violent, ideologically driven methods of the
Hungarian Soviet accords with everything I know about
him. However, aside from attesting to his patriotism and
innate humanity, the affidavit raises a number of questions.
If Captain Fekete and Dr. Fefer were in 'constant personal
contact' with Miklós between 3 October 1918 and 5 August
1919, as the affidavit states, it's far from clear where the
three men spent this period, beginning several weeks
before Austria-Hungary sued for an armistice. As Miklós
was seriously injured at some point in the closing months
of the War, it's conceivable that the men met in a hospital or
a nursing home while undergoing treatment, and that they
remained together in the same medical facility until as late
as 5 August 1919.

However, it's much more likely that Captain Fekete, Dr.
Fefer and my grandfather were already living in Balatonfüred by early October 1918 and that they became acquainted
there, staying on in the resort throughout the bloody and
turbulent months that lay ahead. On the day that Count
Mihály Károlyi formed a radical, left-leaning government
in Budapest at the end of October 1918, and throughout the
spring and summer months of 1919 while Béla Kun's Soviet
administered strong doses of revolutionary socialism to
a terrified and uncooperative 'patient', Captain Fekete,
Dr. Fefer and my grandfather may have met to exchange
news and gossip and to play *ulti*. If I'm right in supposing
that the three reserve army officers became acquainted in
Balatonfüred, then they must have been discharged from

active service at some point *before* 3 October 1918, whether on account of ill health, age, or other factors.

As Captain Fekete and Dr. Fefer signed the affidavit in Balatonfüred in April 1940, it's likely that the two men had continued to live in the town, with their families. By contrast, following the collapse of a brief, ill-conceived business venture in the early 1920s, Miklós left Balatonfüred and settled in Budapest where he met and married my grandmother Etelka in August 1924, finding employment as a *csapos* in his father-in-law's overstaffed bar.

Detestation of Béla Kun and the Soviet wasn't confined to Cécile Tormay and her upper-class friends, or to men like my grandfather who loathed extremism and gratuitous violence. The revolutionary government in Budapest succeeded in alienating almost every segment of Hungarian society with a raft of spectacularly ill-judged policies. The regime's rejection of land redistribution, in favour of establishing agricultural co-operatives, disappointed hundreds of thousands of poorer peasants and agricultural labourers who had hoped that the new government would give them land to relieve their plight.[12] Strict curbs on the activities of the churches alienated religious-minded Hungarians, while sweeping programs of nationalisation were bitterly resented by those affected, who saw them as little more than state-sponsored theft. At the same time, worsening shortages of food and other consumables, particularly in the cities, exasperated everyone.

Writing from exile in Vienna, Vilmos Böhm, who had been one of the leading figures in Hungary's Soviet regime, ruefully acknowledged that the country's workers, who had assumed they would enjoy 'more food, better housing, better clothes and less work' with a revolutionary government in power, became disillusioned when 'the very opposite happened'.[13] At the same time, Hungary's bourgeoisie were dismayed by the unprecedented challenge to their social and economic privileges. In her diary, Cécile Tormay alleges that many of Budapest's better-off residents were appalled by a decree requisitioning private bathrooms on Saturdays, so that children from working-class families would have an opportunity to bathe.† Tormay fulminates against this supposed intrusion into the sacrosanct domestic arrangements of middle- and upper-class households by 'proletarian rabble' and bemoans the fact that the hosts were required to provide hot water, towels, and soap, at their own expense, for the use of their socially disadvantaged 'guests'.[14] People of all social backgrounds hated the Communists because of their habitual resort to violence and intimidation to achieve their ends, but it was military defeat at the hands of Romania that finally dislodged Béla Kun and his Communist associates from power, forcing Kun and several senior comrades to seek sanctuary abroad, initially in Vienna and subsequently in the Soviet Union.

While Kun's revolutionary government had been preoccupied with consolidating its domestic authority, Czech and Romanian armies had launched military offensives against Hungary in spring 1919.[15] Czech troops had seized a tranche of Hungarian territory in the north, including the important mining and industrial city of Miskolc. In April, a large Romanian army had begun to advance from the east. Despite initial success, particularly against the Czechs, Hungary's hastily expanded and reorganised armed forces proved incapable of rolling back the Romanians. In the first week of August 1919, Romanian troops entered Budapest without encountering significant resistance.[16]

† I can find no trace of the alleged decree, cited by Tormay, in the Collection of Decrees published by Hungary's Ministry of the Interior. See *Magyarországi Rendeletek Tára* 53 (1919).

Romanian troops patrolling Budapest, 1919

In her final entry in *An Outlaw's Diary*, dated 8 August 1919, Cécile Tormay claimed to have witnessed high-spirited 'young Jewesses' sitting in taxicabs with officers of the occupying Romanian army. 'How quickly they have made friends! And how happy they seem!' Tormay rails against the anonymous and almost certainly fictitious young women.[17]

Like Dezső Szabó in *The Village That Was Swept Away*, Tormay is anxious to instill in her readers' minds the image of the Jew as rootless, self-interested, and unpatriotic, although I'm quite certain that no one in my family would have been indifferent to the news that Romanian troops had seized control of Budapest. Miklós and Ágoston — together with well over 300,000 of the Empire's Jewish subjects — had fought in the War. Of that number an estimated 40,000 had died, while tens of thousands, including my grandfather, had been seriously injured. For my relatives, as for most ordinary Hungarians, Romania was viewed as a mortal enemy, opportunistically taking the side of the Allies and mounting a military offensive against Austria-Hungary in August 1916.

However naïve it may seem in retrospect, my family, like the overwhelming majority of the country's Jews, considered themselves loyal and patriotic Hungarians. Short of formally relinquishing their Jewish faith and converting to Christianity — like great-uncle Jenő who married a Catholic — my family had embraced almost every aspect of Hungarian culture by the early years of the twentieth century. Aside from my great-grandmother Jerta, whose mother tongue was German, everyone in my family spoke and even thought in Hungarian. They cultivated Hungarian manners, including in matters of dress, read Hungarian newspapers (that is, if they bothered to read newspapers at all), supported Hungarian football teams and, if men, they served with pride, or at least uncomplainingly, in the *Honvéd*. As a matter of course, my relatives ate the same food as other Hungarians, including pork, that quintessentially Hungarian meat. Somehow, though, this wasn't enough, particularly for such self-appointed custodians of the Hungarian soul as Dezső Szabó and Cécile Tormay.

For the celebrated authors of *The Village That Was Swept Away* and *An Outlaw's Diary*, Jews would always remain a race apart, incapable of forming true or enduring attachments to the societies in which they lived. The Hungarian verses fervently penned by my great-aunt Szerénke before her untimely death, Ágoston's lifelong dedication to Hungarian football, Etelka's perfectly-pitched rendition, in Hungarian, of selections from the light operatic repertoire, the injuries that Miklós, Ágoston, and other relatives sustained while fighting for Austria-Hungary in the Great War, Jenő's conversion to the Catholic faith and his marriage to a devout Catholic woman, none of this was enough to persuade Dezső Szabó or Cécile Tormay — who was herself of German descent — that my family had earned the right to be considered Hungarian.

8

How my great-grandfather Adolf may have sold a picture postcard to a celebrated Indian poet

I never saw him sitting or standing up', says my mother, when I ask her about Adolf, her paternal grandfather. As a young child, aged five or six, she frequently accompanied her father on Sunday visits to his elderly parents. At the time, Adolf and Teréz were living with their youngest son, Jenő, and his family in a simple peasant house a short distance from Budapest.

Rabindranath Tagore in Balatonfüred, 1926

My mother, who had spent her entire life in the Hungarian capital, vividly recalls her shock on first realising that the floors inside her uncle's house consisted of bare earth. Refinements such as floor tiles or wooden floorboards were considered an unnecessary extravagance by Uncle Jenő and Aunt Margit, whose lives were ruled by the constant need for frugality. Throughout these family visits Adolf would lie in bed, scarcely moving.

Although my mother wasn't aware of it at the time, Adolf's wife Teréz was dying of cancer. While Adolf would almost certainly have scoffed at the use of such new-fangled medical terms, it's quite likely that his immobility was the result of clinical depression. After a life marked by extraordinary energy, optimism, and determination, Adolf had seen almost all of his cherished business ventures fail, while his wife had been diagnosed with an incurable tumour. It's hardly surprising that Adolf, who was in his sixties by then, couldn't rouse himself from his torpor.

Adolf was already on the cusp of middle age by the time he had saved up enough money to quit his job as a typesetter in Budapest and relocate to Balatonfüred. Here, according to family legend, Adolf started a number of small businesses, including a printing works, a local newspaper, a small giftshop, and the town's first open-air cinema.

Balatonfüred must have seemed an ideal location to an aspiring businessman like Adolf. Forty-eight miles long and up to eight and a half miles wide, Lake Balaton, affectionately known amongst Hungarians as the 'Hungarian sea', attracted increasing numbers of visitors during the course of the nineteenth century. The construction of railway lines along its southern and northern shores greatly facilitated access from Budapest and the provinces, encouraging many middle- and upper-class families to spend part or all of each summer by the lake.

Although there are numerous other resorts dotted around Lake Balaton, many of them former fishing villages that adapted enthusiastically to the influx of tourists, Balatonfüred enjoyed an unrivalled reputation by the turn of the twentieth century. Many of Hungary's leading politicians, actors, and writers mingled in the resort each summer. Lujza Blaha, the 'nation's nightingale' and a supremely popular actress, bought a substantial neo-classical villa in Balatonfüred in 1893, to which she returned each year. Mór Jókai, Hungary's foremost novelist of the nineteenth century, a sort of Central European Sir Walter Scott, purchased an imposing property in the town where he spent much of the summer months writing, entertaining guests, and indulging his passion for gardening. One of Jókai's most famous works, *Az Aranyember*, or *Man of Gold*, was written in Füred during the space of just eight weeks.

The construction of a sanatorium in Balatonfüred further swelled the number of visitors. Built on the site of a thermal baths whose medicinal properties had long been recognised, the sanatorium specialised in the treatment of ailments of the heart. When Adolf moved to Balatonfüred, before the outbreak of World War One, the spa already enjoyed an international reputation.

The Sanatorium in Balatonfüred, 1928

The celebrated Bengali poet Rabindranath Tagore was a patient at the sanatorium during the time that my great-grandfather lived in the town. Tagore, a recipient of the Nobel Prize for Literature, had been taken ill in Budapest in

1926. On the advice of doctors, the venerable poet travelled to Balatonfüred accompanied by his wife, a physician, and his private secretary.[18] Tagore, whose health was soon restored at the sanatorium, arranged for the planting of a lime tree in the municipal gardens as a mark of his gratitude. He also wrote some graceful verses in the hospital's visitors' book: 'When I am no longer on this earth, my tree/ Let the ever-renewed leaves of thy spring/ Murmur to the wayfarer/ The poet did love while he lived'.

Although I can't be certain, it's quite possible that the Nobel Laureate visited my great-grandfather's little giftshop, situated immediately opposite the sanatorium in the lobby of one of Füred's best-known hotels, to buy postcards to send to family and friends. Tagore may even have whiled away some of the evenings at Adolf's open-air cinema, enjoying comic films starring the likes of Charlie Chaplin and Buster Keaton. One of Chaplin's finest silent comedies, *The Gold Rush*, was released the previous year. Perhaps it was screened in Balatonfüred while Tagore was staying there?

Despite the resort's numerous attractions for holiday-makers as well as for those seeking medical treatment, Balatonfüred couldn't escape the cumulative effects of external events. As late as the summer or autumn of 1913, when Adolf was already established in the town, no one could have foreseen that the heir to the Habsburg throne would be assassinated in Sarajevo by a hot-headed young Serbian nationalist and that the incident would lead to a cataclysmic war. Even after the armies of Austria-Hungary commenced large-scale military operations against Serbia, the Empire's wisest and most far-sighted generals, politicians, and diplomats never imagined that the rapidly widening conflict might drag on for several years, destroying the Empire and exhausting both Austria and Hungary, as well as several other European powers. And who could have guessed that, as a result of the peace settlement concluded after the War, Hungary would emerge shrunken and humiliated, stripped of over seventy percent of her former territory and more than sixty percent of her pre-war population?

In addition to the War and the almost equally catastrophic peace that followed in its wake, Adolf failed to anticipate the Great Depression, which plunged Hungary even further into economic misery in the early to mid-1930s. With soaring unemployment, drastic cuts in wages, and the forced sale of tens of thousands of small-holdings by peasant farmers who could no longer service their debts, a growing number of shopkeepers and small businessmen, including my great-grandfather, faced the unsettling prospect of bankruptcy.[19] One by one, Adolf was forced to close his businesses until only the little giftshop remained. At some point in the early 1930s, perhaps after Teréz had fallen gravely ill, Adolf decided to retire, leaving his elder daughter Ilona and her husband Tódor to run the shop.

In Dezső Szabó's novel *The Village that was Swept Away*, Félix Gutman is the archetypal Jewish businessman of anti-Semitic cliché. Avaricious, rapacious, and unscrupulous, his physical appearance is every bit as unsavoury as his personality:[20]

> The few hairs that were left on the stubbly head of this podgy, diminutive man were already grey. His neck was bloated and enveloped in fat, while his physiognomy was stamped with the cunning yet fearful smile that is so frequently encountered in the East. Yet, in his eyes, there was an unwholesome craving, an insatiable appetite.

Before the War, he had been a travelling salesman repre-
senting a major manufacturer. But now he had made
millions, many millions, through a thousand different
stratagems. He was one of the most dazzling successes of
the War… whom everyone hated, everyone despised, yet
whom no one dared to oppose.

Dezső Szabó's fictional creation is a profiteer who has
accumulated a vast fortune through the unexpected and
frequently illegal opportunities presented by the First
World War. Szabó's crudely anti-Semitic storyline conveys
the message that Gutman and, by inference, all of Hungary's
Jews, have exploited the War and the suffering of their
fellow countrymen to advance their personal interests and,
wherever possible, to amass enormous and undeserved
wealth. Gutman, who is clearly intended to be emblematic
of Hungary's Jews, is ambitious, cunning, resourceful, and
a perpetual outsider. For Szabó, Jews are dangerous inter-
lopers whose overweening ambition is only matched by
their lack of patriotism and their inveterate cowardice.

As far as I'm aware, no one in my family has faced accusations of profiteering or of unscrupulous business dealings.
With the possible exception of Adolf, none of my relatives
has even shown much aptitude for business. Certainly, no
one has managed to accumulate great wealth. In contrast to
the Rothschilds, the Guggenheims, and the Ephrussis, my
family's talent has more often expressed itself in producing
unsuccessful businessmen.

The bustling and apparently flourishing bar over which
my great-grandfather Bertalan presided, in Budapest's
fashionable Jókai *tér*, was sold off soon after his death to
settle a large unpaid tax bill. Several members of my family,
including Etelka, Miklós, and Katica, were thrown out of
work as a result.

My great-grandfather Adolf

Ilona and Tódor, for their part, never attempted to expand their 'business empire' beyond the little giftshop founded by Adolf in Balatonfüred. The business provided the couple with a modest income as well as simple accommodation behind the shop.

Out of everyone in my family, Miklós, my maternal grandfather, was almost certainly the least suited for a career in business. Miklós possessed neither commercial acumen nor personal ambition, while he seems to have lacked a capacity for ruthlessness. By nature, my grandfather was neither assertive nor ingratiating. When strings had to be pulled, during the course of his adult life, it was invariably my grandmother Etelka who found them, seized them, and tugged at them with all of her customary vigour and single-mindedness.

My grandfather's business ventures after World War One were short-lived and spectacularly ill-judged. In contrast to his father Adolf, who saved up for years so that he could leave paid employment and start a number of small enterprises, Miklós seems to have preferred the security and routine of a salaried job. Desperation rather than an entrepreneurial spirit or a craving for wealth prompted my grandfather to become a businessman.

My mother says that, throughout his service in an infantry regiment in World War One, Miklós had looked forward to returning to his former employment as an insurance clerk in Budapest. But the injuries he sustained in the final, desperate months of the War, which left him with severely limited dexterity in his right hand as well as other disabilities, dictated the future trajectory of his working life. No longer able to write legibly — a prerequisite for office workers in an era before the keyboard rendered penmanship virtually obsolete — Miklós had to give up all thoughts of clerical work.

Perhaps it was on the advice of well-meaning friends or business associates of Adolf, who was living and working in Balatonfüred by this time, that Miklós decided to become an agent in the grain business. Some years later, finding himself unemployed once more, he leased a small *kifőzde*, or luncheonette, in a run-down neighbourhood of Budapest. With his pronounced limp and his almost useless right hand, my grandfather was peculiarly ill-suited for the role of the luncheonette's only waiter, while my grandmother's barely rudimentary cooking skills meant that, although she did most of the shopping and cleaning, the couple had to hire a cook.

The closure of the *kifőzde* in 1932 marked the conclusion of my grandfather's short-lived business career. Now married and the father of two small children, his only remaining income was a small invalidity pension. Miklós had to find a job as quickly as possible. Predictably, it was my grandmother Etelka who took the initiative, paying a call on an old schoolfriend whose husband was now an executive of an oil company with its head office in Budapest.

For Etelka, who had once enjoyed much the same cossetted, middle-class lifestyle as her former schoolfriend — fine clothes, a handsome apartment, private music lessons, a hectic social life, and the services of a live-in maid — it must have been an awkward and uncomfortable encounter, emphasising the vast social and economic gulf that now separated the two women. However, my grandmother's urgent pleas for help found a sympathetic response. Shortly afterwards, Miklós was offered a job as a petrol-pump attendant at the oil company's filling station in Csepel. Despite the low wage, the menial nature of the work, the unsocial hours, and the constant exposure to the elements, neither my mother nor my uncle ever heard their father complain or suggest that he intended to look

for another job. Although there is a widely held belief that
Jews are good at business and at making money, my family
triumphantly demonstrated time and again and at no little
personal cost that such generalisations are hopelessly false.

Peasant children, Hungary, 1920

'There were twenty-five Jewish families in this village before
the War,' Simon tells me in fluent Hungarian.[21] It's spring
2006, and we are sitting in the principal room of Simon's
house, with its peeling wallpaper, utilitarian furniture, and
large, old-fashioned television set. Simon's wife, a cheerful
Romanian woman who is at least twenty years younger
than Simon, serves me pancakes and unpasteurised buffalo
milk that she has heated on the stove.

Simon was born in 1922 and has lived in this house for
most of his life. For some years now he has been the only Jew
in Ocna Şugatag, a rambling village in Maramureş county,
Romania, not far from the town of Sighet and the Ukrainian
border. Most of the Jews from Simon's village died in the
Holocaust or left shortly after the War, unable to reconcile
themselves to the loss of relatives, neighbours, and friends,
many of whom perished in Auschwitz-Birkenau. Other

Jews from the village emigrated during the Communist era when the Romanian government permitted Jews to resettle in Israel in return for a hefty payment in US dollars.

Before the War, Jews weren't settled exclusively in cities; across Eastern Europe they formed an integral part of the life of villages, rural settlements, and small provincial towns. They earned a living as shopkeepers, peddlers, carpenters, shoemakers, farmers, loggers, innkeepers, schoolteachers, tailors, mill owners, carters, lawyers, doctors, and vets.[22] Simon tells me that his father was a butcher, while several other Jews in Ocna Şugatag worked as carpenters or shoemakers. It seems that every Jewish man in the village had a trade. 'Everyone lived well,' Simon says, although I can't help wondering whether his memories of good and contented Jewish lives in Ocna Şugatag before the War are really accurate or whether they have mellowed with the passage of time.

Novels and short stories written before World War Two are a rich source of information about the lives of Jews settled in villages and country towns in Eastern Europe before the Holocaust. In Lajos Nagy's novel *Kiskunhalom*, published in 1934, the eponymous village of the title contains no fewer than four cemeteries, to accommodate Catholics, Evangelicals, Calvinists, and Jews. 'Those who in life mixed together, working the same land, drinking in the same bar are now neatly separated from one another,' writes Nagy.[23]

With a wealth of statistical and other information more commonly found in works of ethnography than in novels, Nagy presents his readers with a detailed description of life in the village. Although a work of fiction, *Kiskunhalom* is an authentic portrait of countless Hungarian villages of the period. So it's worth noting that one of *Kiskunhalom*'s most prominent citizens is a successful Jewish farmer, Artur Weisz.

My great-grandfather Adolf

The proprietor of a small estate comprising a little over two hundred acres, Weisz lives in the nearby village with his wife. Their house is set in the midst of a substantial, well-tended garden with an abundance of fruit trees, a large vegetable plot, and outbuildings that accommodate a variety of livestock, including cattle.

Weisz visits his estate regularly, both to inspect the crops and to keep an eye on his farm workers. During one such visit, at harvest time, Weisz is shown eagerly examining the grains of wheat that the over-worked threshing machine is spewing into waiting sacks: 'That's the main thing, the grain. He grabs handfuls of the grain once, twice, fingering it, weighing it in his hand, letting the grain run between his fingers.'[24]

Unlike the experienced and knowledgeable Artur Weisz, who has lived all his life in the village and who knows as much as any peasant or estate manager about farming and crops, my grandfather Miklós lacked any real connection with the land. As a neophyte grain agent in the early 1920s, Miklós could never hope to gain the respect of men like Artur Weisz or of the peasants. It's hardly surprising that, in his business dealings with farmers, my grandfather was outwitted and outmaneuvered at every turn.

Grain agents like my grandfather bought wheat or corn directly from farmers, frequently peasants with just a few acres of land. Deals were often struck long before the crop had even been harvested, particularly if a peasant farmer urgently needed to raise some cash. Ideally, an agent had to have a thorough knowledge of farming, particularly of soil conditions and crops. An understanding of human nature — peasants are not necessarily more honest, reliable, or straightforward than anyone else — was also an advantage, while basic business skills, particularly the ability to buy cheap and sell dear, were indispensable. Miklós, who had spent most of his life in Budapest and who had never shown the slightest entrepreneurial flair, was deficient on all of these counts.

After little more than a year, says my uncle, Miklós grew weary of trudging round the dusty villages and farmsteads of Somogy county, south of Lake Balaton, striking unprofitable deals with peasant farmers. As his borrowed capital slowly dwindled away, Miklós was forced to acknowledge that he would never earn a living in the grain business. Instead, he decided to return to Budapest where, through mutual friends, he met my grandmother, Etelka. As mentioned in the previous chapter, the couple married in August 1924, and Miklós' father-in-law Bertalan found him a job in his bar.

After returning from active service in World War One, my grandfather never managed to translate his school-leaving certificate, his diligence, and his dependability into a proper career or a satisfactory income. Miklós' proven aptitude for bookkeeping, for something called 'commercial geography', and for 'commercial correspondence' in Hungarian, German, and French — to name just a few of the subjects my grandfather studied for his *érettségi* — failed to land him a white-collar job. For the remainder of his life, particularly after the forced closure of his father-in-law's bar, money was almost always a problem, even for basic necessities such as food. My mother recalls that her parents squabbled frequently about their finances, particularly at night when they thought that the children were sleeping.

Slowly, Miklós came to understand that an ability to pass exams doesn't necessarily mean very much in real life. With its unexpected challenges and its occasional life-threatening hazards, real life never seemed to bear much resemblance to the rational, well-ordered world depicted in

my grandfather's textbooks on bookkeeping and commerce
that had so appealed to him as a schoolboy.

9

The family Weisz

Whenever she spoke of them, which was often, my grandmother liked to portray her family as genteel and respectable. So Etelka rarely mentioned her older brother Ármin, or her wayward sister Katalin, whom everyone knew as Katica. Their behaviour offended my grandmother's unyielding sense of propriety, so she excised them from her reminiscences about growing up in Budapest in the early years of the twentieth century. Ármin and Katica were airbrushed out of Etelka's reverential narrative, which seems a shame.

Family portrait, 1912

From some of the stories I've heard — admittedly accounts differ — Katica comes across as a decent and likeable woman, particularly to anyone with a modern outlook. In her way, Katica was an early and instinctive feminist, or perhaps a sensualist. She scorned, at least for a while, the stifling moral conventions of her day. By contrast, as

I can recall, my grandmother was inclined to be prudish. Etelka was uncomfortable with sexuality except as a means, necessary but regrettable, of procreation. My grandmother liked and approved of children.

In all, Etelka had three sisters and two brothers. Etelka's youngest sister, Szerénke, whom we encountered previously, died when she was barely out of her teens. Unlike Szerénke, who was slender, delicate, and resolutely high-minded, my great-aunt Katica was short and tremendously fat as well as surprisingly vain about her appearance. There is no evidence that Katica took the slightest interest in any of the arts, in contrast to Szerénke and Etelka, or that she continued her education beyond the minimum considered necessary by her parents. Aside from a slight genetic predisposition, my great-aunt's bulk may have been the result of a life-long addiction to chocolate. Katica was the fleshly embodiment of Oscar Wilde's immortal line: 'I can resist anything except temptation'.

After World War One, Katica worked in the family-owned *kocsma* alongside Etelka and her father Bertalan. Aside from serving the customary range of alcoholic beverages — wines, beers, and *pálinka*, a local spirit made from plums, apricots, quince apples, pears, or cherries — the *kocsma* offered its customers simple snacks. These would almost certainly have included slabs of white bread thickly spread with pork dripping and sprinkled with paprika, plump *hurka* or black pudding, and meatballs generously flavoured with garlic and herbs. Situated on Jókai *tér*, close to the Ferenc Liszt Music Academy, the Opera House, and the shops lining Andrássy *út*, as well as numerous apartment buildings, basement workshops, and commercial premises, the bar was often packed. Men would stop off each morning on their way to work for a beer and a generous shot of *pálinka*. Often the same men would call in on their way home and perhaps at lunchtime as well. For many of Bertalan's customers, including the lonely, the unhappily married, and those in need of respite from cramped, noisy apartments and boisterous children, alcohol helped to dull the pain of life.

A kocsma in Budapest, 1930

During the years that Katica worked in the family-owned bar there were frequent rumours about her private life. It was said, although you shouldn't believe every bit of tittle-tattle, that Katica took a succession of lovers from amongst the men who frequented the bar. It's even been hinted that some of her lovers were married, although there's no hard evidence to back up such gossip. Everyone in the family agrees that Katica enjoyed the company of men and that, in their turn, men found Katica agreeable and good-humoured. I can picture Katica now, her pudgy hands resting on the polished mahogany counter of the *kocsma*, laughing heartily at a rather risqué joke that she's just been told by one of the regular customers. It's an image that would have made Etelka, my prudish grandmother, blanche!

As you might expect, after an interval of over sixty years, memories of Katica's personality, aside from her sexual mores, differ. According to my mother, Katica was kind-hearted, jolly, resourceful, and industrious. But my uncle recalled that Katica was inclined to be cantankerous. He told me that she was lazy and that she didn't like to get up in the mornings. Perhaps my uncle acquired some of these unflattering opinions, which may of course be fully warranted, from my grandmother. Etelka and Katica didn't get on.

Following the death of my great-grandfather Bertalan Weisz and the forced sale of the bar to settle a large unpaid tax bill, Katica didn't look for a job straight away. Instead, she moved in with another of the Weisz sisters, Ilona, whom everyone knew as Ilus. After some months, Katica was compelled by lack of funds to accept a job as a housekeeper. Her employer, 'Uncle' Vilmos, was a jeweller who lived in an apartment with his bed-bound, diabetic wife.

Unlike Katica, who was considered selfish and lazy as well as dissolute by some members of the family, everyone seems to have had a favourable opinion of Ilus, who was said to be straightforward, kindly, hardworking, and unpretentious. Ilus, who had trained as a hairdresser, ran a small salon on Szinyei Merse *utca*, in a respectable if slightly unfashionable district of Budapest. She rented a small apartment nearby.

Ilus didn't marry until she was twenty-nine years old, and she and her husband never had children. According to my uncle, the couple's childlessness may have been due to an injury sustained by Ilus' husband during the First World War. He was said to have been thrown from his horse, landing awkwardly and severely damaging his testicles.

Although Ilus never said anything directly to anyone, there's a feeling in the family that she didn't marry out of love. Perhaps Ilus dreaded the prospect, common enough in the 1920s amongst women of her generation, of remaining a spinster. Due to the massive casualties sustained by the Hungarian army — with fatalities amounting to well over half a million men — there was a shortage of potential husbands after the War.

As things turned out, Ilus didn't live to a ripe old age anyway, so she needn't have worried about becoming an old maid. She died of a ruptured bowel in June 1938, just months before the outbreak of World War Two. In a way, and looking at things in hindsight, you might even say she was lucky.

If my grandmother's relationship with Katica was overshadowed by differences of temperament and outlook, her relationship with Ágoston, the younger of her two brothers, was to become increasingly strained, particularly after Etelka accepted a marriage proposal from my grand-father. In Ágoston's view, which was not entirely without foundation, Miklós was an unsuitable match for his sister as he patently lacked the means to support a family. In addition to the fact that Miklós was partially disabled and had already shown that he had no head for business, my grandfather possessed neither professional qualifications nor even a trade. Ágoston rightly judged that Etelka was unlikely to enjoy a life of luxury or pampered idleness with Miklós, although even he never imagined the numbing poverty that his sister and her children would have to endure.

Some years before Etelka met Miklós, Ágoston had urged his sister to accept an offer of marriage from a lovelorn doctor who lived in the same apartment building as Etelka and her parents on Nagymező *utca* in Budapest. My grandmother's refusal to marry the doctor on account of his congenital deformity — she had been concerned not so much by the unsightliness of the doctor's hunchback as by the possibility that the condition could be inherited by any children he might father — had infuriated Ágoston, resulting in serious and lasting damage to relations between the two siblings.

A large, physically imposing man, who became increasingly corpulent in middle age, Ágoston had strong features and a commanding presence. As previously mentioned, his all-consuming passion was football. Initially associated with Fradi, first as a player and later as an official, a series of anti-Semitic incidents at the club in 1919 prompted Ágoston to join Fradi's arch-rival, MTK Budapest,[25] where he was appointed manager of the youth team, also serving on several committees of the Hungarian Football Federation. Despite these onerous and time-consuming responsibilities, Ágoston's income from football was irregular, at best, obliging him to take various mundane jobs to support himself. Ágoston's daughter Ági once told me that her father worked as a book-keeper and as a salesman, selling everything from handicrafts to encyclopaedias.

Angyalföldi football team, 1927

In many ways, Ágoston's bearing and tastes, if not his family origins, were those of a Hungarian gentleman. Aside from the necessity of earning a living, Ágoston had no interest in commerce, let alone in accumulating wealth. First and foremost, Ágoston was proud of having so many friends and acquaintances amongst the country's sporting elite and of his work for MTK and the Football Federation.

Ági once showed me a black and white photograph, taken some time in the 1920s, at a social event organised by MTK. Ágoston is standing in the very centre of a row of loose-limbed, athletic young men wearing dinner jackets. Amongst his comrades, he looks the very epitome of masculine pride. Football was always much more than just a game for Ágoston and, in the end, you could say that football saved his life.

As for my grandmother's other brother, Ármin, my mother recalls that she often heard Etelka refer to him as *linkóci*, a disparaging term that translates roughly as 'unreliable' or 'spivvish'. My grandmother's dismissive attitude towards Ármin may have had as much to do with his personal life as his working habits. According to those who remember him, Ármin was obsessed with cars, initially working as a driver and subsequently trading in second-hand motor vehicles. Although it's said that Ármin was inclined to be lazy and that he never really applied himself, he earned enough money to rent a small apartment on Kresz Géza *utca* in the popular Újlipotváros district of Budapest.

From the doorway of Ármin's apartment building a short stroll would have brought him to the banks of the Danube, with its stunning views of Parliament and of the castle district across the river in Buda, as well as of an endless cavalcade of ferries, pleasure craft, and ponderous, slow-moving barges. If Ármin had chosen to proceed along Szent

István *körút*, the most obvious route, he would have passed the ornate façade of the *Víg Szinház* or Comedy Theatre, although Ármin was not noted for taking an interest in the arts.

At the foot of the *körút* or boulevard, Ármin would have come to Margit *híd*, one of several bridges linking sprawling, commercial Pest with the hills and elegant villas of Buda. A few hundred metres along the bridge, just a single stop on the tram, would have brought Ármin to Margitsziget, an island named after the saintly and ascetic daughter of a thirteenth-century Hungarian monarch. Rejecting offers of marriage from the sovereigns of Bohemia and Poland, Margit chose to spend much of her brief life in a convent on the little island.

The swimming baths, Margitsziget, 1935

By Ármin's day, Margitsziget catered for the recreational needs of Budapest's middle classes. Aside from a park that ran the entire length of the island, there was a miniature zoo, kiosks selling beer, spicy sausages and pretzels, a restaurant with a brightly-clad Gypsy orchestra, tennis courts, swimming pools, and a spa where visitors could wallow like walruses in the warm, medicinal waters. The small fee levied for entrance to the island, which was abolished by the Communist administration after the Second World War, wouldn't have worried Ármin, although it served as an all-too-powerful deterrent for my grandparents, who didn't have money to spare for luxuries, however modest.

Margitsziget, 1943

It was Ármin's matrimonial life, rather than his business dealings, that attracted most gossip within the family. There were persistent rumours that his wife, Ella, encouraged her husband to slap her around. It was whispered that Ella was sexually aroused by these acts of conjugal violence. This explanation, which conveniently allows Ármin to escape the charge of being a wife-beater — except in the most literal sense — is difficult to reconcile with the general feeling that Ármin's marriage was unhappy. My uncle Bertalan remembers that the couple didn't sleep in the same room even though the apartment was small. He says that Ella took the bedroom while Ármin habitually slept on a collapsible cot-bed that was erected each night in the hallway. Their children, Guszti and Marci, occupied the apartment's only other room. These details of the family's sleeping arrangements suggest that Ármin's intermittent assaults on his wife, to which everyone attests, are unlikely to have been an expression of mildly deviant, if consensual, foreplay.

In one of Chekhov's most celebrated plays, *Three Sisters*, true happiness is elusive. In the end, each of the sisters can only achieve a measure of contentment by letting go of her dreams. Masha, the tempestuous and talented middle sister, learns to accept life with her dull, doting husband, a schoolmaster, following the end of her passionate love affair with an army officer. For Olga, the eldest, thoughts of marriage and of romance finally fade as she comes to terms with the fact that she is destined to remain a spinster and the principal of a school for girls. Even Irina, the youngest, who yearns for the excitement and sophistication of Moscow, comes to accept that her life will take a different and much less glamorous course.

Chekhov seems to be saying that, while it's only human to nurture dreams and ambitions, for most of us happiness lies in accepting what we already have or what lies within our grasp. Rather than striving for perfection or for the extraordinary we should learn to love the simple, the imperfect, the ordinary. Or, to put it another way, Chekhov is telling us that real happiness isn't *over there* in another place or another time but *right here* under our noses. Of course, Chekhov, whose brief and eventful life was neither simple nor ordinary, didn't take his own advice.

Like the tarnished heroines in Chekhov's play, my grandmother and her surviving sisters, Ilus and Katica, had their fair share of dreams. My grandmother often told me that, as a teenager, she had longed to become a professional singer specialising in the light operatic repertoire, performing night after night before adoring audiences. One of Budapest's most celebrated music halls, the *Fővárosi Orfeum*, was located on Nagymező *utca*, just a short distance from the Weisz family's apartment. Each time she passed the theatre, Etelka must have lingered before billboards advertising operettas performed by local and foreign theatre companies, shows featuring aquatic displays, silent films, and exotic singers from as far away as India and the Levant.

Etelka always maintained that the only reason she had failed to pursue a musical career was the implacable opposition of her mother, who retained old-fashioned notions of upper-middle-class decorum. Apparently, Jerta considered the designation 'female singer' little more than a euphemism for 'prostitute'. While my grandmother's devotion to her parents was legendary, I can't help wondering whether her ambitions may not have been stymied by other factors. My grandmother's singing voice, as I can recall, was thin and warbly when she was in her seventies. Even as a young woman, Etelka may not have impressed music teachers or impresarios quite as much as she liked to suggest in later life. Alternatively, it's conceivable that my grandmother was forced to abandon her musical ambitions because of her father's mounting financial problems. Bertalan, who had to find work in the family-owned bar for several of his children once they reached adulthood, may have baulked at the tuition fees demanded by Budapest's elite music conservatory.

The notion that Jerta refused to countenance any of her daughters appearing professionally on stage is also difficult to reconcile with the fact that she seems to have had few, if any, qualms about Etelka and Katica working in the *kocsma*. Dispensing alcohol to raucous and frequently inebriated customers, many of whom must have tried to flirt with the female bar staff, was hardly more dignified than appearing in light operas composed by such luminaries of the form as Johann Strauss and Franz Léhár.

If my grandmother faced disappointments in her professional life, she also had to deal with ones of a more private nature. Etelka once confided to my mother that, several years before she met Miklós, she had fallen in love with a young man whom she had met through mutual friends in Budapest. The young man was Jewish, of good family, and had wanted to marry Etelka. However, when it became clear that Bertalan wouldn't be able to provide the couple with a proper dowry, the young man had succumbed to parental pressure and had abandoned his suit: despite a fine apartment on Nagymező utca, elegant clothes, bountiful hospitality extended to a wide circle of relatives and friends, as well as other signs of apparent wealth, my great-grandfather's income from the bar was much less substantial than many people supposed.

10

For richer, for poorer

Attila József

'No mother, no father,' begins one of Attila József's most famous poems, *Tiszta Szívvel* (*With a Pure Heart*), written in March 1925 when the poet was not yet twenty, several years after the death of his mother. In the original Hungarian the verses have a rhythmic, staccato quality, like the urgent beat of a drum. Here is the poem in my own translation:

No mother, no father,
No homeland, no God,
No cradle, no shroud,
No lover's name to call out loud.

It's three days since I last ate
A meal or a crust of bread,
The only thing I have to sell
Is my twenty years, my youth, myself.

If no one wants what I have to offer,
I can steal and rob to earn a dollar,
The Devil himself can claim my name,
With a pure heart I'll kill and maim.

They'll catch me and they'll hang me high,
In holy ground my body will lie,
Poisoned grass will start to grow
On my beautiful heart in the earth below.

With a Pure Heart was published in a newspaper while Attila József was still an undergraduate student in Szeged University's Faculty of Arts. The poem was praised by many of Hungary's leading literary figures, including Hugó Ignotus, the long-serving editor of the influential literary journal *Nyugat*.

József's youthfully iconoclastic poem, which dismisses the idea of a 'homeland' or of a 'God' and which, at least on a literal construction, suggests that the poet would be willing to steal or murder to sustain himself, provoked outrage in conservative circles. After reading the verses, Antal Horger, one of József's professors, summoned the young poet to his office. In the presence of witnesses, Horger informed József that, although he would be permitted to continue his studies, he would not be awarded a teaching certificate by the university. Brandishing a copy of the newspaper in which József's poem had been published, Horger is said to have exclaimed: 'You can't become a schoolmaster if you have notions such as these!'[26]

The visceral anger and nihilism that represent such striking features of József's poem were the product of his unhappy, impoverished childhood as well as of his troubled temperament, which psychiatrists today would almost certainly diagnose as a personality disorder. József was just three years old when his father, a soap factory worker, abandoned the family, compelling his mother to place József temporarily with foster parents in the country while she worked. The future poet, the most important to have emerged in Hungary since Endre Ady, spent his days as an underage swineherd. József was seven before he was reunited with his mother and began his schooling.

The plight of József's mother, who supported herself and her children from her meagre earnings as a washerwoman, was the inspiration for some of Attila József's finest poems. In *Anyám* (*My Mother*), written after her death, József offers a moving portrait. After washing and ironing all day at the house of a well-to-do family, József's mother returns home towards evening with a small saucepan containing her supper. The food is a gift from her employer. Attila József, who was as proud as he was poor, rails at this supposed act of charity from a family who, unlike his own, could sate their hunger whenever they chose. The final stanza of *Anyám* is almost unbearably poignant:

> She was already a little stooped from laundry work,
> Maybe that's why I hadn't noticed she was still a young woman,
> In her dreams she wore a clean apron
> And the postman always greeted her on his rounds.

In her poverty and hopelessness, József's mother serves as a potent metaphor for inter-war Hungary, which was known throughout Europe as 'the land of three million beggars,'[27] a figure corresponding to approximately a third of Hungary's population at the time. Conditions in rural Hungary were notoriously harsh. Writing in the *American Ethnologist*, Martha Lampland notes that 'nearly two-thirds of those engaged in agriculture [in Hungary] were landless or owned only one to two acres, not enough to provide a family with a year's subsistence.'[28] As Jószef's poem *Anyám* vividly illustrates, the lives of the urban poor in inter-war Hungary were often almost equally bleak.

Following the Wall Street Crash of 1929, conditions in Hungary deteriorated sharply as the Great Depression impacted on almost every sector of the country's already fragile economy.[29] The value of Hungary's agricultural exports collapsed, one in seven factories ceased production, while levels of unemployment amongst the country's industrial workers soared to thirty per cent. As many as 60,000 Hungarian smallholders, burdened by debts they were no longer able to service, were forced to sell their land. Half a million agricultural labourers lost their livelihoods and as many more were obliged to accept starvation wages.

In his novel *A Boldog Ember* (*The Happy Man*), Zsigmond Móricz offers some insight into the desperation and incomprehension of ordinary people in Hungary caught up in the Great Depression. First published in serial form in a newspaper, the *Pesti Napló*, beginning in 1932, the novel consists of a series of reminiscences by a peasant, György Joó, whose home lies in a village in the bleak northeast. Following crop failure and the plummeting price of wheat, Joó travels to Budapest in the hope of obtaining work. Previously, whenever he had come to the capital city, Joó had been offered employment almost immediately. Now, Joó is dismayed to discover that, however hard he looks, there's no work to be had:[30]

These days it's impossible just to scrape a living. I thought to myself, I'll go up to Pest and earn myself some money, but even that's out of the question now. There's no work to be had any more in Pest. Before? When I came up to Budapest in the past? Why, as soon as I arrived at the *Keleti* [railway] station and started to make my way along Rákóczi *út* I'd be stopped by a gaffer with the words, 'young man, do you want a job?' 'Of course, I want a job!' 'In that case come with me', and I'd be put to work right away. I remember that we built a large house on Kinizsi *utca*. I worked there until Christmas. In those days they were desperate for workers. Now? Why, I've been here for eight days. I've made inquiries everywhere, amongst all my old acquaintances. All the big firms that I've worked for in the past have gone out of business. I even called on his Honour the Deputy [Member of Parliament] but he couldn't help me either. There's no work.

Unemployed men, Budapest, 1942

I don't know if Miklós ever read Attila József's poetry or the prose works of Zsigmond Móricz. Given my grandfather's lowbrow tastes, it seems unlikely. Even so, Miklós would have been all too familiar with the numbing poverty and despair that József describes in many of his verses and that Móricz depicts in both novels and short stories.

Although Miklós grew up in a lower middle-class household where there was almost always enough food of some kind, he would have encountered abject poverty amongst the poorer peasants and agricultural labourers of Somogy county while working as a grain agent. In Budapest, Miklós would have witnessed destitution and despair on the streets of the capital, particularly in the chaos and economic dislocation following World War One. In those years, poverty and hopelessness enveloped Hungary like a tattered shroud.

After the forced sale of his father-in-law's bar in Jókai *tér*, Miklós experienced poverty at first hand, first as the proprietor of a failing luncheonette and, latterly, as an underpaid petrol pump attendant. Yet, unlike Attila József, Miklós didn't complain or rail against his fate. My grandfather always tried to make the best of things.

Etelka, aged about 60

'*Kisemberek*,' mutters my grandmother. 'Little people'. Despite Etelka's disparaging remark — which thankfully our English hosts don't understand — my grandmother is giving every appearance of enjoying herself. Etelka has been smiling fixedly for most of the day, nodding with apparent appreciation as a plate loaded with bland and unappetising English foodstuffs is placed before her: pork sausages, slices of dry roast turkey, stuffing, roast potatoes, bread sauce, cranberry jelly, watery, over-cooked vegetables that have been denied even a fleeting contact with potentially contaminating foreign substances such as olive oil and garlic. In our hosts' kitchen, reminiscent of the England of the 1950s, the only permitted condiments are pepper and salt.

When everyone is already alarmingly full our hostess brings in a Christmas pudding, accompanied by jugs brimming with white sauce and cream. '*Kisemberek*' is my grandmother's tiny, unnoticed act of revenge.

It is December 1975 and Etelka, my parents, and I are spending Christmas Day with my fiancée and my future in-laws at their home in Croydon. My grandmother's acerbic remark shows that she has lost none of the snobbishness and hauteur acquired during her comfortable, bourgeois childhood in Budapest, despite the poverty she experienced as an adult after marrying my grandfather. Although Etelka has never said anything to me directly, I'm well aware that she would have liked me to marry someone from an affluent, upper-middle-class British family, with a house in Hampstead or Putney, rather than the daughter of an insurance clerk living in unfashionable Croydon.

Although my fiancée is completing an MA in English Language and Literature at a top British university, and although she will go on to qualify as a lawyer, it's clear that Etelka is unimpressed by her family, who are neither well off nor highly educated. In my grandmother's damning estimation, my fiancée's parents are lower middle-class.

Given Etelka's ingrained snobbishness, how am I to make sense of the fact that she married Miklós? After all, Miklós, like my future father-in-law, had been an insurance clerk before he was conscripted into Austria-Hungary's armed forces in World War One. Neither man seems to have been particularly ambitious or interested in making money. Like Cyril, my kindly future father-in-law, Miklós had modest tastes and limited expectations of life. Both men were essentially quiet, good-natured, and family-oriented. Of the two, my future father-in-law was the more cultured, with his deep love of classical music and German literature.

Although Etelka wouldn't have cared to admit it, Miklós was a *kisember*. He possessed neither capital nor professional qualifications and, by the time he met my grandmother, he'd already demonstrated a woeful lack of commercial acumen, having failed as an agent in the grain business. So why would a proud and snobbish young woman like Etelka have agreed to marry an almost indigent semi-invalid like my grandfather?

Despite my mother's vehement protestations, I can't help thinking that Etelka may not have been madly in love with Miklós when she married him. Although my grandfather was trim and not at all bad looking, he lacked the accomplishments, social status, and — let's be frank — income that would have impressed my grandmother. Perhaps most importantly, Miklós had grown up in a family that, despite all of Adolf's prodigious efforts to make a success of his various business ventures, was generally poorer and less socially aspirational than Etelka's. My grandfather's modest, self-effacing mother, Teréz Mándl, offers a striking contrast to Jerta Rudolfer, his exacting and formidable future mother-in-law. Although I'm sure Etelka considered

Miklós handsome and personable, I suspect that she accepted his offer of marriage for reasons that had little to do with notions of romantic love.

Etelka was thirty-one years old when she married Miklós, in August 1924, at the Dohány Street Synagogue in Budapest. By that point, the sound of the biological clock ticking in Etelka's ear must have been deafening. Etelka and her parents would have known that, if she rejected Miklós' proposal of marriage, she might be condemned to a lonely and childless spinsterhood. Or, at best, she might hope to marry a hard-pressed widower who needed someone to run his household and to help him raise his children.

As previously mentioned, well in excess of half a million Hungarian soldiers had died in the War. An additional 1.4 million were wounded, out of a total pre-war population of a little over eighteen million.[31] Young women of Etelka's generation were left with a restricted choice of marriage partners, particularly if their parents couldn't provide them with a generous dowry. Etelka, who was thickset, bordering on plain and already thirty years old when she was intro-duced to Miklós by mutual acquaintances, knew that she couldn't afford to be unduly choosy.

Unlike the hunchback doctor, whose advances she had spurned some years earlier, there was every reason to believe that Miklós would father healthy children who would not be afflicted with an unsightly deformity. In addition, Miklós was courteous, cheerful, not afraid of hard work and, in a country renowned for heavy drinking, abstemious. In contrast to my strong-willed grandmother, Miklós was mild-mannered and easy-going, generally content to let the course of his life be dictated by others. Perhaps most impor-tantly, for Etelka would not have dreamed of upsetting, let alone alienating, her parents, Miklós was Jewish, although completely uninterested in matters of religion. Etelka could have done worse for herself, although her brother Ágoston continued to have strong reservations about Miklós as a potential husband for his sister.

As for Miklós, it's hard to avoid the conclusion that, in marrying Etelka, he was at least partially motivated by the knowledge that his father-in-law would offer him a job. In 1924, Bertalan Weisz's bar still gave every appearance of flourishing. Miklós would have assumed that he could look forward to secure, long-term employment with his father-in-law, although both the wages and the prospects would have been modest.

Even if I'm right in thinking that my grandparents may not have been in love when they married, the bond that developed between Etelka and Miklós was real enough. In a photograph, taken during an outing in the Buda hills with Miklós' sister Klára and her family, Etelka and Miklós are side by side. My mother, who is sitting cross-legged in the centre of the little group, is adamant that the photograph was taken in the summer or autumn of 1935 and that she was nine years old at the time. Her brother Bertalan, whom almost everyone in the family called Öcsi, or 'little brother', is wearing glasses, his elbow brushing against my mother's knee.

Although the photograph is a little indistinct, Miklós is immediately recognisable. He is lolling on the grass, on the far right of the little family group, next to his wife. Miklós and Etelka are wreathed in smiles. Unlike Klára and her husband Imre, who are sitting some distance apart from one another, Miklós is leaning towards his wife, their shoulders almost touching. Anyone looking at this photograph would be in no doubt that Miklós and Etelka were a close and affectionate couple, even though their relationship was marred by constant financial worries and by Etelka's neurotic and groundless conviction that Miklós was plotting serial infidelities. Etelka was convinced that women found Miklós irresistible and that he would cheat on her without a moment's hesitation if he had the chance.

My mother is close to tears. 'They were devoted parents,' she says. 'While I was growing up I felt particularly close to my father. He was always so cheerful and good-natured.' By contrast, Etelka was inclined to be stricter as well as an inveterate worrier.

'Tell me about Klára and Imre,' I ask, in part to distract her. 'What were your aunt and uncle like? What became of them?'

I knew that, like my grandparents, Klára and Imre had very little money. The family survived on Imre's modest earnings as a shop-assistant. Klára, his wife, suffered from tuberculosis and wasn't well enough to work.

'It was terrible,' recalls my mother. 'Klára couldn't hug or kiss her own son. Whenever she came close to Gyuri she held a handkerchief over her mouth to avoid infecting him.'

In the photograph Klára, with her dark hair, glasses, and Semitic features looks unmistakably Jewish. She couldn't have passed for a gentile even if she'd wanted to.

'What became of them?'

My mother sighs. All she knows is that Klára and Imre died during the War. Somehow, though, Gyuri survived.[†]

'Gyuri was lucky,' says my mother, matter-of-factly. After the War, an uncle of Gyuri's, who owned a successful business in Balatonlelle, returned from serving in an auxiliary labour battalion reserved for Jews and other 'undesirables'.[32] After learning that his wife and children had perished in Auschwitz he adopted Gyuri, who had no one else to care for him.

According to my grandparents' wedding certificate, Etelka and Miklós were married at the Dohány Street Synagogue in Budapest on 17 August 1924. Dr. Gyula Fischer, the Chief Rabbi of the reformist Neologue movement, officiated, perhaps at the insistence of Jerta, Etelka's snobbish mother. There would almost certainly have been a reception of some kind after the wedding ceremony, maybe at a homely *vendéglő* or in one of Budapest's more modest hotels. I can picture Etelka's father Bertalan surveying the assembled guests as he proposed a toast to Miklós and Etelka. Despite Hungary's serial misfortunes — defeat in the Great War, the despotic excesses of Béla Kun's Soviet Republic, the Jew-baiting and random terror unleashed by 'patriotic' Hungarian elements after Kun and his associates fled and, finally, the catastrophic and humiliating peace settlement forced upon Hungary by the Allied Powers — I'm sure that Bertalan would have declared that he had every confidence in the future happiness of the young couple. After

---

† According to official records, compiled after the War, Klára died of heart failure on 8 January 1945, in Budapest's Jewish ghetto. Just ten days later, Soviet troops liberated Pest, including the ghetto. At the time of her death, Klára was 36 years old. In all likelihood, her husband, Imre, who did not survive the War, perished in the ghetto or died while serving as an auxiliary labour serviceman.

all, Admiral Horthy had been installed as Regent, while the shrewd and far-sighted Count István Bethlen had been appointed as Prime Minister.[33] Now that law and order had been restored, Hungary could get on with rebuilding its shattered economy and with forging a modern, forward-looking country, fully in keeping with the spirit of the new century.

With his limited education, positive outlook and unshakeable faith in the civilized virtues of the Hungarian nation, how could my great-grandfather have conceived that, barely four years later, a sudden and unprecedented collapse of share prices in the US would trigger a series of events in Europe that would threaten not just the happiness but even the lives of his entire family? Such things were beyond the bounds of Bertalan's imagination.

The death of Bertalan Weisz in 1926 at the age of seventy-four precipitated a bitter and protracted conflict within the family. According to my mother, Bertalan's adult children fell out over the inheritance, although once back taxes had been paid on the *kocsma* there was precious little left.

'Look at this,' says my mother, indicating a photograph of her grandfather aged about sixty. Bertalan is smartly dressed, almost a dandy. His luxuriant handlebar moustache has been expertly waxed and trimmed. My great-grandfather must have cut an impressive figure as he strolled along the boulevards of Budapest. His elegant clothes and dignified air would have lent his *kocsma* a certain cachet, although I can't help wondering whether Bertalan's speech may have betrayed his patchy education and provincial origins.

'Do you see that watch chain?' asks my mother, pointing to the photograph. Like most middle- and upper-class men of that era, Bertalan wore a pocket watch. The watch was connected to an ostentatiously long gold chain that, in turn,

was attached to his waistcoat. Bertalan clearly wanted to convey the impression that he was a person of substance even though, in reality, he was often perilously close to bankruptcy.

'When my grandfather died, Etelka and Katica somehow managed to get hold of his watch chain. They divided it between themselves, without leaving Ágoston anything. He never forgave them.'

This is my mother's version of events, and it's plausible. With a partially disabled husband, who would have had great difficulty in finding another job if the *kocsma* were sold, Etelka must have been consumed with anxiety about her family's future. Acquiring half of her father's gold chain would have helped to allay her fears, if only for a little while. As for Katica, opportunism and indolence as well as a casual disregard for social mores would easily explain her apparent willingness to deprive Ágoston, as well as Ármin and Ilus, of their shares of the gold chain. Grossly fat, nearing forty, lacking professional qualifications or a trade and without a husband or even a steady boyfriend to support her, Katica could well have reasoned that she needed as much of the gold chain as she could lay her pudgy hands on. By contrast, Ágoston, although far from rich, always had a job of some sort and was a popular and well-regarded official of the MTK, while Ilus was a hairdresser with her own premises, however modest. Even Ármin, although incorrigibly idle, made a decent enough living selling second-hand motor cars.

After I became acquainted with Ágoston's daughter Ági, visiting her several times at her cottage-style home in Wekerletelep, in Budapest's Nineteenth District, I finally brought up the subject of her grandfather's gold chain.

'Let me show you something,' Ági says, smiling. After rummaging in a chest of drawers in her bedroom, she returns triumphantly to the sitting room, a length of gold chain in her hand.

'This can't be from Bertalan's…'

'Oh yes it is!' Ági assures me. 'The gold chain was divided into three equal parts between Katica, Etelka, and my father. My father had a pocket watch too. He kept it on this chain.' Why Bertalan's other children, Ilus and Ármin, were denied any share of their father's gold chain remains a mystery, along with the fate of the watch itself.

Ági proceeds to paint a strikingly unflattering picture of my grandmother and of Katica. In contrast to her father, Ági tells me, the sisters had behaved in a selfish and unscrupulous fashion.

'Dad was the type of person who never wanted to keep anything for himself,' she says, ignoring the fact that her father had chosen to keep a third of the gold chain while Ilus and Ármin apparently received nothing. 'He always wanted everything to go to his family. I saw that for myself. If he only had one forint left and I asked him for an ice-cream he would give me all his money.'

By contrast, says Ági, after the death of Bertalan, Etelka and Katica showed themselves to be grasping and self-serving. 'The women wanted to have practically everything and told my father that he should consider himself lucky if they gave him anything at all!' she says, relying on what her father had told her.

While Ági's version of events may be true, it's also possible that Ágoston gave his daughter an edited version of the facts that showed him in a favourable light. A strong and forceful personality and a graduate of the *Ludovika*, Hungary's Westpoint, Ágoston had been an army officer in World War One. It seems unlikely that a man such as Ágoston would have allowed Etelka and Katica to bully him out of his share of their father's modest estate.

'Dad wanted to keep the *kocsma*, maybe invest some money in it to make it more profitable, but his sisters sold the place without his knowledge.'

'How could they do that?' I ask, taken aback.

'You're a lawyer. You know that the law is riddled with loopholes. Everything depends on how good your lawyer is. Dad was away at the time, fighting in the War. Perhaps his sisters told the lawyer who was handling their father's estate that they had been authorised to represent Ágoston?'

Although I've only known her for a short time it's become clear to me that, like her father, Ági is not the sort of person who can be easily persuaded to change her mind. However, her account of the illicit sale of the family-owned bar strikes me as implausible. While Ágoston served as an infantry officer in World War One, his father Bertalan only died in 1926, fully eight *years* after the end of hostilities. So Ágoston couldn't have been away 'fighting in the War', as

Ági suggested, when the bar was sold following Bertalan's death.

Ági's conviction that the law is hopelessly porous, with innumerable loopholes that render laws virtually meaningless, reflects a common assumption amongst laymen. But that doesn't mean Ági is right. It's simply not credible that the two sisters, Etelka and Katica, could have sold the bar without Ágoston's knowledge or consent. There are things that even the shrewdest and most able lawyers can't accomplish.

If Ágoston told Ági that he had opposed the sale of the bar and that his sisters had tricked him he may have been trying to convince himself, as much as his daughter, that he wasn't responsible for the sudden and precipitous decline in the family's fortunes. In losing the *kocsma* the Weisz family lost not only a potentially valuable economic asset but also an important marker of their middle-class identity.

Ágoston, as we've seen, became increasingly involved in the management of his cherished football club MTK, also serving on various committees of the Hungarian Football Federation. Although far from rich, his income from football and from other sources grew to the point where he could afford to rent a three-room apartment in a popular district of Pest, even hiring a live-in maid. As related previously, Katica, after some months of self-imposed idleness living with Ilus, accepted a post as housekeeper for a jeweller, 'Uncle' Vilmos, and his invalid wife. Within a few years, the modestly affluent jeweller was widowed, leaving him free to marry Katica, whose life was utterly transformed.

Out of all the children of Adolf and Jerta Weisz, only my grandmother Etelka endured abject poverty. After a disastrous spell running an unprofitable luncheonette with her husband, Miklós took a job as a petrol pump attendant. Having enjoyed a comfortable, upper-middle-class lifestyle while she was growing up in the spacious family apartment on Nagymező *utca*, Etelka now found herself relegated to the swollen ranks of Hungary's urban poor.

11

Lunch

In Zsigmond Móricz's story *Lunch*, an old-fashioned country squire entertains important visitors from Budapest. The squire's cook prepares luncheon for the party, which includes several local dignitaries, amongst them the chief of police, an archdeacon, and the *alispán* or sub-prefect, who is in charge of local government in this fictional backwater. The squire has assembled this Chekhovian cast as a mark of respect for his visitors from the capital, who are here on some unspecified matter of business.

Zsigmond Móricz

Móricz is uninterested in the squire's financial affairs or in the men from Budapest. They are not identified by name, while their physical appearance, clothes, and speech are sketched out in only the most perfunctory fashion. By contrast, Móricz's description of the drawn-out meal, with its apparently endless succession of substantial courses, is leisurely, detailed, and sensual. Móricz leads us right up to the edge of the squire's long, old-fashioned dining table and allows us to savour each of the hearty, intoxicating dishes as it is brought in.

Lunch, which was originally published in 1930, is neither a thriller nor a murder mystery.[34] No one is held hostage, dies, or encounters paranormal phenomena. There are no confrontations with aliens from outer space, or last-minute reprieves from the jaws of huge and implausibly malevolent sharks. There isn't even a hint of romance or eroticism in Móricz's tale to engage the reader's interest. The only female character in the story is the squire's sturdy, middle-aged cook, who is scarcely the stuff of conventional sexual fantasy. Hollywood would find Móricz's story deficient, lacking even the basic elements of a compelling screenplay. All that happens in *Lunch*, insofar as anything happens at all, is that a group of people, all of them conservative, comfortably off men in their middle or later years, come together in a manor house on the Hungarian *Alföld* to talk, drink, and, most importantly, to eat.

Despite the absence of incident Móricz's story is remarkable, if only for the extraordinary quantity and variety of food consumed by the squire and his gluttonous friends. Unlike the abstemious visitors from Budapest, the locals treat the gargantuan lunch, comprising eleven substantial courses, as if it were nothing out of the ordinary. Beginning with glasses of potent *pálinka*, taken in an anteroom, the squire and his guests adjourn to the dining room where, like seasoned troops taking up well prepared positions, they settle themselves in their chairs, tuck their napkins in at their collars ,and resolutely pick up knives, forks, or spoons as required, ready to do battle with a succession of dishes, each of which is laid before them in stupefying quantities:

Slow-cooked broth of beef and fowl

—∞—

Bone-marrow served with toast

—∞—

Roast beef with redcurrant sauce

—∞—

Mutton stew with marrow

—∞—

Pork stew with green beans

—∞—

Roast duck with stewed fruits

—∞—

Slices of goose liver with risotto

—∞—

Chicken in paprika sauce

—∞—

Catfish fried in breadcrumbs

—∞—

Noodles with curd cheese made from ewe's milk

—∞—

Fresh cherries

—∞—

Black coffee

Móricz's story is a paean to the cholesterol-laden delights of the Hungarian kitchen, a reckless, almost suicidal inversion of the Mediterranean diet. In traditional Hungarian cooking, of the kind favoured by the squire and his cook, vegetables, fruit, nuts, pulses, and even fish are relegated to a minor, supporting role while meat of every description, soured cream, and saturated animal fat (mostly pork or goose) occupy centre stage. 'If I could, I'd eat meat with meat,' a middle-aged Transylvanian Hungarian once remarked to me. '*Hús hússal*'.

Móricz's frame — photographs of the writer show a stocky figure with a lugubrious moustache — suggest that he may have been following the old writer's adage to write about what you know. Móricz knew and loved food perhaps, in part, because his childhood and adolescence were punctuated by periods of hunger. But if Móricz adored eating plentifully and well, he also knew what it meant to go without. In his memoir *Életem regénye* (*The Story of my Life*), a substantial chapter is entitled 'Hunger'.[35]

Móricz recalls, in the book, that his early childhood, spent in the village of Tiszacsécse in the far east of Hungary, was idyllic. Food as well as affection was lavished on the young child. His mother Erzsébet was well educated, the daughter of a Protestant clergyman. His father Bálint came from a peasant family. Determined, energetic, and hard-working, Bálint Móricz was imbued with ambition and entrepreneurial zeal.

For some years, Móricz's family prospered. But a steam-powered threshing machine, which Bálint bought on credit, very nearly ruined him. The threshing-machine exploded while it was being repaired, leaving the family with substantial debts and few means of repaying them. Móricz's parents were obliged to sell their house, land, and other assets in Tiszacsécse to satisfy their creditors and to provide themselves with sufficient capital to start a new life elsewhere. Eventually, the family relocated to the village of Prügy, 144 kilometres to the west. Here, Bálint found work as a carpenter while Erzsébet supplemented her husband's modest income with her earnings as a seamstress. For two years, while his parents established themselves in Prügy,

Móricz was sent to live with his penurious, ill-tempered grandmother, who occupied a gloomy, one-room house in a distant village. In stark contrast to the comfortable family home that Móricz had known in Tiszacsécse, his grandmother's house had virtually no furniture other than a bed, while the tiny kitchen contained nothing but a stove and two small cooking pots.

Móricz experienced real, if occasional, hunger only after he was reunited with his parents; on some days there was simply no food of any description in the family home. As he notes dryly in his autobiography: 'Bread and everything else that's good [to eat] in the world, all that we didn't have. But we did have furniture'.[36]

The young child's reaction to his family's straitened circumstances was one of shame. Móricz records that he was ashamed of his father because he was no longer able to provide for his family, and ashamed of his mother because of her inability to fulfill a mother's natural role of nurturing her children. He even felt ashamed of himself for having nothing to eat.

Móricz's feelings of self-loathing had been shaped by his experiences at the elementary school he had attended in his grandmother's village. Here, Móricz had copied his classmates in shunning those children who had come to school without any food for the morning break. However innocent or pathetic these children may have appeared to outsiders, they and their parents were viewed by the local villagers as sinful, as potential thieves, and as harbingers of disease. As Móricz explains, these harsh and unforgiving attitudes towards the very poorest members of the community were the product of the tough peasant culture of the Hungarian *Alföld*. Its central tenets — based on the imperative of survival — were hard, unremitting physical labour and almost constant self-denial. For the peasants of the *Alföld*, real, life-threatening hunger, as opposed to occasional periods of belt-tightening, was viewed as shocking, even sinful as it suggested indolence or a culpable lack of thrift. While the squire and his friends in Móricz's story gorge on meat of every description in an orgy of carnivorous consumption, the peasants and agricultural labourers of Móricz's childhood lived in a world of stern rationing:[37]

> As wheat was grown on the Hungarian plain, you could eat bread to your heart's content… But meat was a different matter; meat was strictly portioned out. If you worked on a farm and received your meals there, you were only allowed to eat as much meat as the farmer's wife decided to give you or, if you were a child, as much as your parents doled out — and not one scrap more! It was inconceivable that anyone would ask for more meat if they had already received their allotted portion… Other foodstuffs could be consumed according to their price: more beans than noodles or pasta; more cabbage than beans; almost as much potatoes as bread.

The casual reader may be tempted to conclude that *Lunch*, which was written when the Great Depression was destroying the livelihoods of countless Hungarians, was simply a fiction, a grotesque parody of the selfish, frequently gluttonous behaviour of the upper classes. While the squire and his cronies feasted on the finest meats, in the country at large hundreds of thousands of peasants and agricultural labourers faced desperate poverty. Móricz's story, aside from being an entertainment, is also a morality tale.

Although exaggerated for comic effect, the huge meal consumed by the squire and his cronies was nowhere near as fanciful as might be supposed. In her memoir, Catherine Károlyi, born into a wealthy, aristocratic Hungarian family in the final quarter of the nineteenth century, recalls 'interminable meals' at her family's estate in Tiszadob in the north of Hungary, which are only slightly less extraordinary than the gargantuan lunch in Móricz's tale:[38]

> At Tiszadob an ordinary day's luncheon began with a substantial entrée, followed by fish from the River Tisa — the deliciously crisp *kecsege*, a kind of sturgeon, roasted over an open fire. Then came a main dish, usually beef with three or four vegetables. The fourth course would be a vegetable by itself, asparagus or a soufflé. After that, tart with ice-cream — my favourite was '*bombe á la* Izmet Pasha', first tasted by my parents in Turkey at the table of the Pasha after whom it was named — and then the meal would continue with sweet corn-on-the-cob with butter. We would eat four or five cobs. After this we had cheese and biscuits, and finally melons — delicious, red, juicy water-melons cooled in ice — and, of course, all the other summer fruits too.

For the upper and upper-middle classes in Hungary, the consumption of food often had less to do with nourishment or sating hunger than with the open display of wealth, hospitality, and good taste.

—m—

'We only ate meat once a week,' says my mother, recalling her childhood in Budapest. 'On Sundays, we usually had *Wiener schnitzel*.' Of Viennese origin, as its name suggests, *Wiener schnitzel*, consisting of thin slices of veal or pork that are dunked in flour, beaten egg, and breadcrumbs and deep fried in lard, has long been a mainstay of the Hungarian kitchen. During the rest of the week my mother and her family were reluctant vegetarians, subsisting on stodgy, carbohydrate-packed dishes such as *hamis hús* or 'fake meat': 'Mother would boil potatoes in their skins and then peel them, mashing the potatoes with a fork. Then she'd add salt, pepper, some parsley, and a little beaten egg. With her hands, she'd form small, round balls, resembling meatballs, out of this mixture and deep-fry them in lard.'

Another of the family's staples was macaroni served with a simple sauce made with fried onions, chopped tomatoes, and a little paprika powder. Otherwise, an evening meal in winter might consist of a few slices of toast spread with goose or, more commonly, pork fat, lightly seasoned with garlic. The toast was invariably accompanied by cups of hot lemon tea. In summer, supper was frequently a thick wedge of watermelon, eaten with white bread.

'As a family of four, we used to eat two kilos of bread every day,' says my mother. 'When I tell friends how much bread we ate as children, they're amazed. But we had to fill up on something.' The bread came from the *tejcsarnok*, a grocery store that was willing to sell goods on credit. 'We mostly ate things that we could buy in that shop.'

My grandmother's habit of frying everything in pork fat, as well her readiness to spread it on toast for herself and her family, may surprise some people. After all, one of the most sacrosanct dietary principles of the Jewish faith is the interdiction of the consumption of pork. Day by day, in her little kitchen, my grandmother was subverting one of the Almighty's inviolable commands. All I can say, in my grandmother's defence, is that pork fat was cheap; almost everyone in Hungary cooked with it, including plenty of Jews.

While some Hungarian Jews remained strictly observant, complying with the exacting dietary require-ments of their faith, many of their co-religionists ate pork on a regular basis, including *szalámi*, *kolbász*, *szalonna*, and other processed pork products. In parts of the Hungarian countryside such as Orosháza, the small town on the *Alföld* where my father spent his childhood and teenage years, it was commonplace for Jewish families, like their Christian neighbours, to raise pigs for their own consumption.[39] Although Jews might worship God (or, more properly, G-d) in a different language and in a synagogue rather than a church, many Hungarian Jews would happily sit down to a dinner of knuckle of pork.

Some members of my family, including my grandmother Etelka, continued to think of themselves as religious, however wayward their dietary habits and however infrequent their attendance at synagogue. Others, like my grandfather Miklós, preferred to live a life free of religion and its myriad strictures. After marrying my grandmother in a synagogue, Miklós rejected religion completely, along with the accumulated religious paraphernalia of four millennia. My grandfather happily turned his back on *tefillin* and prayer shawls, on hand-stitched *kippehs* and silver *yads*, along with all of the beliefs and practices associated with them. At the same time, and however paradoxical this may seem, my grandfather continued to think of himself as Jewish.

My mother can't remember Miklós ever talking about his religious beliefs, but she has little doubt that her father was an atheist. 'He never once went to synagogue and I never ever saw him pray,' my mother tells me. 'I think his whole family wasn't religious.'

On *Yom Kippur*, the most solemn day in the Jewish calendar, when Jews are required to spend much of the day at prayer and fast for twenty-five hours, my grandfather was defiant, maintaining his usual routine without deviations of any kind. On Friday nights, when Jewish families gathered around the dinner table for the *Shabbat* meal, Miklós would infuriate my grandmother by refusing to say *Kiddush*, the prayer that the male head of the household is supposed to recite before the meal can begin.

Faced with my grandfather's intransigence, it was left to my grandmother Etelka to try to preserve some sense of the family's Jewish identity. However, even Etelka drew the line at replacing pork dripping with goose fat or butter, both of which would have been far more expensive. For my grandmother, religious interdictions, however weighty and unambiguous, were always superseded by the sacrosanct laws of economics. Fear of indebtedness, or of not being able to feed or clothe her family, far exceeded Etelka's dread of the Almighty and of offending Him by breaching His edicts. My grandmother was confident that, if called upon, she could convince Him that she had behaved righteously.

If Etelka was selective in her religious observances, she was at least consistent in trying to conserve some elements of her Jewish heritage and in passing these on to her children. 'On Friday evenings, my mother would always light a candle and say a prayer,' recalls my mother, even if the simple meal that the family ate bore little resemblance to the elaborate *Shabbat* feasts enjoyed by affluent Jewish families. Once her children were old enough, Etelka insisted that they join her in fasting for twenty-four hours on *Yom Kippur*, despite their father's wayward behaviour.

In the end, all of Etelka's efforts were in vain. While they were growing up, neither of her children showed much enthusiasm for religion, while in old age my mother has begun to show signs of a religious openness or pluralism that would have startled Etelka. For some time, my Jewish mother has taken to praying in a local Catholic church and has been keeping a small vial of holy water in her handbag along with a tiny, plastic effigy of the Virgin Mary, gifts from a devout Catholic friend who'd brought them from Lourdes.

'I remember once, before *Yom Kippur*, my mother bought a hen, a live hen,' recalls my mother. 'She twirled it above her head while reciting a prayer'. But my mother can't remember the words of the prayer or even what the prayer was about. As an exercise in religious education, Etelka's efforts were an abject failure. For my mother, only the image of the startled, indignant fowl remains, and of Miklós sitting impassively at the dinner table, a silent, involuntary bystander.

I wonder if Etelka knew that the ceremony she was performing, which may have originated amongst the Jews of Babylonia, is called *kapparot* and that its object is to transfer sins from man (or woman) to a hapless bird. From an ethical perspective, *kapparot* strikes me as an exercise in moral elision. As for the theological controversies surrounding the practice — the ritual has been regarded with disfavour by prominent Jewish scholars since as far back as the Middle Ages — I'm sure my grandmother was unaware of them. For Etelka, the ceremony was a comforting reminder of her happy Jewish childhood and an opportunity to strengthen her family's fraying links with the faith of their forefathers.

Poverty alone cannot fully account for my grandparents' unsatisfactory diet after the sale of the family-owned *kocsma*, which had provided them with a modest but regular income. Etelka had a limited and imperfect knowledge of nutrition, while her culinary skills, as I can attest, were rudimentary at best. Unlike my paternal grandmother Eleonóra, who always presented me with delicious home-baked pastries whenever I visited her, Etelka cooked solely out of a sense of duty. For Etelka, cooking was a chore, much like sweeping the floor or cleaning the windows. Although she busied herself with her pots and pans and invariably produced meals on time, my grandmother was always impatient for the daily routine of cooking, eating, and washing-up to be over.

At least part of the problem with Etelka's cooking stemmed from the fact that she hadn't been taught how to cook. Until she was well into her twenties, Bertalan and Jerta assumed that their daughter would marry someone of her own class, a man who, if not necessarily rich, was at least comfortably off. In such circumstances, Etelka's role within her future household would have been largely supervisory. Cooking and other menial household chores would have been left to the live-in maid and to other domestic help that Etelka and her husband might choose to employ.

As things turned out, and in part because of her stubbornness in declining an offer of marriage from the hunchbacked doctor, my grandmother ended up with no one to supervise. Once she was married and living with Miklós, there were no maids, cooks, or laundry women to relieve Etelka of tiresome domestic chores. My grandmother had to do everything herself, including painting and decorating their one-room, rented apartment on Szinyei Merse *utca*, where they moved with their young children after Miklós was hired as a petrol pump attendant in the early 1930s. My mother says that, with his lame leg and almost useless right arm, my grandfather would have struggled to wield a paintbrush.

In many ways Etelka's adult life, after she married my grandfather, came to resemble a game of snakes and ladders. But the ladders were always somehow just out of reach, and the snakes were long, slippery, and almost constantly underfoot.

My grandparents' unbalanced diet, in which proteins and vitamins made only an occasional guest appearance, was also linked to the fact they lived in Budapest, in a cramped apartment, rather than in a village house with its own plot of land. There were no trees or bushes to provide seasonal fruits, nuts, or berries, and no chickens scratching in the yard to lay eggs. There was no earth in which to plant potatoes, onions, peppers and cabbages. Everything that my mother and her family ate had to be paid for.

Even so, neither ignorance nor geography was as important as the lack of money in dictating my grandparents' monotonous and unhealthy diet, in which a starchy triumvirate of bread, macaroni, and potatoes featured most prominently. Like millions of other Hungarians, then as now, my grandparents suffered first and foremost from poverty, a chronic and debilitating condition that even Budapest's finest doctors haven't been able to cure.

Hungarian literature of the first half of the twentieth century offers a vivid portrait of poverty across the country. Many of the nation's finest writers wrote about poverty, often in their most celebrated works. Zsigmond Móricz's short story *Hét Krajcár* (*Seven Pennies*), published in 1908, is a good example of this genre. The narrator, in recalling his impoverished childhood, begins the story with the following words:[40]

> The Gods have arranged matters well so that even the poor man can laugh. You won't just hear crying and wailing coming from the slums but plenty of laughter too. It's a fact that the poor often laugh when they have good cause to cry.

Seven Pennies, which is told from the viewpoint of a young boy, follows his mother as she searches every drawer and corner of their one-room hovel for a few stray coins. She needs the money to buy a bar of soap with which to wash the family's clothes. In order not to alarm her infant son, the mother pretends that the quest for the seven *krajcár* is a game. By the time she has enough money — the final penny is a gift from an itinerant beggar — it's grown dark. As there's no fuel for the only oil lamp in the house, the mother realises that she won't be able to wash any clothes after all. The woman bursts into a fit of laughter, whereupon grim humour turns into tragedy. The young boy is suddenly aware that his mother, whom he adores, is coughing up fresh, warm blood.

The poet Attila József, whom we encountered in an earlier chapter, wrote copiously about poverty. It was a subject that, even more than Móricz, he understood at first hand. In a fine poem entitled *Éhség* (*Hunger*), written in 1922, József describes a typical bucolic scene, but without any of the cloying romanticism that is commonplace amongst poets writing about the countryside. *Éhség* is an exercise in social realism as well as a work of simple, unaffected beauty. Watching agricultural labourers pausing for lunch during harvest-time, József is struck by their exhaustion and by their 'dirty, sweat-sodden shirts'.[41] Although he chooses not to make the point explicitly, it's clear to the reader that the labourers' simple meal, which contains no meat or protein of any kind, is unlikely to satisfy their hunger or restore their strength: 'Today, their lunch is bread and cucumbers/ They eat their food carefully, so as not to waste a crumb.' The fact that the workers eat their food 'carefully, so as not to waste a crumb' tells us everything we need to know. For these impoverished agricultural labourers, most of whom would have been *napszámos* hired for the duration of the harvest, even bread and cucumbers are in limited supply.

Unlike Attila József, my grandfather wasn't a poet. He lacked the magical power to transmute hunger, cold, or other discomforts of the body or soul into art. Miklós wasn't an alchemist of the human condition. In my grandfather's clumsy, untutored hands, hunger remained hunger, cold remained cold, fear remained pure visceral fear. For Miklós, suffering wasn't alleviated by the consolations bestowed on artists and poets.

My grandfather differed from Attila József in another respect. Unlike the rebellious, strong-willed poet, my grandfather was dutiful. Whether as a son and brother, as a schoolchild, as an insurance clerk, as an infantry officer in the Great War, as a petrol pump attendant, or as a husband and father, my grandfather unfailingly did his duty. Even in November 1944, at the very end of his foreshortened life, my grandfather remained dutiful. Without protest, Miklós joined the long, weary column of Jews trudging under armed escort from Budapest towards the border, where only exhaustion and death were waiting for them. Even if he hadn't been lame, it would never have occurred to my grandfather to break the rules and to try to escape.

12

The perils of smoking a pipe

Etelka kept in touch with many of her old friends even after she married and had a family of her own,' says my mother. Unlike Etelka, most of her friends had married well and led comfortable, sometimes pampered lives.

My mother, aged 6, with her younger brother Bertalan

'I particularly remember Bianka,' recalls my mother. 'Bianka was one of Etelka's oldest friends. She was so pretty and always wore beautiful clothes!'

Bianka and her husband, Dr. Zsigmond Hegyi, a successful gynaecologist, lived in a handsome, modern apartment building on Jászai Mari *tér*, close to Margit Bridge, in a highly sought-after part of Budapest.

'Dr. Hegyi had his consulting room in the apartment,' says my mother, who often accompanied Etelka on visits to her friend. 'Their apartment was enormous! At least, that's how it seemed to me at the time. There must have been as many as three or four rooms!'

My mother recalls that Bianka, who was childless and came from a well-to-do family, once received a bicycle from her doting husband. 'She used to ride it in the park on Margitsziget. In those days, bicycles were still comparatively rare. They were very expensive.'

Etelka and Bianka continued to see one another regularly after they were married. However, it was tacitly agreed between them that their husbands wouldn't join them on these occasions; Dr. Hegyi and my grandfather Miklós inhabited different worlds.

As a rule, the two old friends would meet in Bianka's spacious apartment, with its riveting views of the Danube and the Buda hills. Sensitive and easily moved to tears, Bianka refused to come to the tiny flat overlooking a gloomy courtyard that was Etelka's home for most of her married life. 'It would break my heart to see one of the Weisz sisters living in a one-room apartment!' Bianka is said to have told my grandmother. 'I simply can't bring myself to visit you there!'

Yet, for my grandmother, that one-room apartment was a huge improvement over her former living quarters. For well over a year, she and her family had occupied a cramped, windowless space behind a luncheonette in the shabby Józsefváros district of Budapest. As mentioned earlier, following the enforced sale of the family-owned bar my grandparents had taken out a lease on a *kifőzde*. Etelka and Miklós had somehow convinced themselves that the luncheonette would provide them with a regular income as well as basic but adequate accommodation.

'There were rats, enormous rats, and it was very damp!' exclaims my mother with an involuntary shudder, recalling the family's dismal living quarters behind the *kifőzde*.

My uncle, a civil engineer who has spent a lifetime designing everything from bridges to house conversions, offers a more dispassionate description. 'The luncheonette was located on József *utca* in a working-class district of Budapest,' he tells me. 'It was on the ground floor, with access directly from the street. There were six round tables with chairs.'

Bertalan pauses to draw me a diagram of the *kifőzde* on a notepad as we sit in his immaculate kitchen in a quiet Toronto suburb. My uncle's hand is unsteady due to the onset of Parkinson's.

'Behind the dining area there was a narrow, windowless corridor leading to the kitchen, the courtyard, and a toilet. That's where we slept, in the corridor.'

Registering my surprise, Bertalan smiles. To my uncle, I must seem hopelessly privileged and naïve, much like Etelka's childhood friend Bianka.

'We slept on folding beds that were stowed away in the basement every morning. Bedding and clothes were stored in cupboards in the passageway.'

Bertalan doesn't remember the rats or the damp that appalled my mother. But he recalls that, each afternoon, he and my mother had to sit quietly at one of the vacant tables in the *kifőzde* until the last customer had finished his meal and left. Only then could Miklós and Etelka set about erecting the family's rickety beds in the passageway.

My uncle says that Miklós waited on the tables while Etelka helped to prepare the food, as well as doing most of the cleaning and shopping. A middle-aged woman who had some experience of catering was employed to do the cooking. Etelka's comfortable upper middle-class upbringing as one of the Weisz sisters had prioritised singing lessons over the acquisition of domestic skills. It had left my grandmother ill-prepared for running a professional kitchen.

Reflecting on this short and unhappy episode in my grandparents' lives I find myself recalling a popular British television series, *Dragon's Den*. The program, which has been running since 2005, is based on a simple but compelling formula. A succession of aspiring entrepreneurs, some of them hopelessly unready or self-deluding, try to persuade the 'dragons' to invest in their fledgling businesses. The 'dragons' are hard-headed, plain-speaking, successful businessmen and women. They grill the budding entrepreneurs mercilessly, a frequently excruciating spectacle that accounts for much of the program's voyeuristic appeal.

In my mind's eye I can picture my grandparents standing uncomfortably before the dragons in the full glare of the television lights. Miklós is shuffling his feet, his eyes downcast. Etelka, more assertive and naturally self-assured, meets the dragons' unsparing gaze.

'So, tell us about your business idea?'

'We want to open a *kifőzde*.'

'What are your qualifications? Can you cook?'

My grandfather, incapable of dissimulation, says nothing, looking despairingly at my grandmother.

'Yes, I can cook,' Etelka lies.

'Have you ever cooked professionally?'

My grandparents are silent.

'And who'll wait on the tables? You?' asks one of the dragons, dismissively, jabbing a finger at my grandfather. In order to take up their positions in front of the dragons, my grandparents had to walk a short distance, no more than a dozen yards, across the room. The dragons immediately noticed my grandfather's pronounced limp. At least Miklós could console himself with the thought that he'd managed to conceal the condition of his right arm. Due to injuries sustained during the Great War, the arm was almost useless, quite incapable of holding a heavy tray loaded with plates of food.

'What about the competition?' asks one of the dragons. 'Have you checked to see how many luncheonettes, restaurants, and taverns there are in the district already and how busy they get?' My grandparents start to look rattled.

'Have you given any thought to the state of the economy right now?' asks another dragon. Hungary, like much of Europe, was already reeling from the effects of the Great Depression.

'Do you really think that this is a good time to be opening a luncheonette, with unemployment spiralling and those still in work facing massive wage cuts?'

By now, even my grandmother is tongue-tied, staring miserably at the floor as, one by one, the dragons declare emphatically that they won't invest one single *fillér* in such an ill-conceived business venture.

My grandparents should have listened to the dragons and to the friends and relatives who urged them to show caution. Instead, Etelka and Miklós suppressed any doubts that they may have had, heeding a siren-like inner voice that enticed them forward onto the rocks of failure and despair.

After a little over a year my grandparents had to acknowledge that, however hard they worked, the *kifőzde* would never provide them with a satisfactory income, even though their expectations were modest. There were weeks when the business barely made a profit, while Etelka's legs had become painful and swollen as a result of having to stand for hours on end each day in the pokey kitchen. The couple were also concerned for their children who, like their parents, slept in the damp, windowless corridor.

'When my parents decided to give up the *kifőzde*, Etelka paid a visit to an old schoolfriend whose husband had become an executive at the Hungarian Petroleum Company,' says my mother. As related previously, Etelka begged her friend to speak to her husband about Miklós. Within a matter of days, my grandfather received an offer of employment as a petrol pump attendant at the Company's filling station in Csepel.

With his high-school leaving certificate, his knowledge of several foreign languages, his work experience as a clerk in the insurance industry, and his wartime service as an army officer, Miklós was hugely over-qualified for a menial position as a pump attendant. But jobs were scarce, particularly for anyone with a disability; Miklós accepted the offer without a moment's hesitation. With the prospect of a small but regular wage, as well as my grandfather's modest war invalidity pension, the family could begin to look for an inexpensive apartment.

'Etelka heard about a vacant third-floor flat on Szinyei Merse *utca* in the Terézváros district,' says my mother. 'The rent was just about within her budget.' With its apartment buildings, workshops, and commercial premises, Terézváros (named after the Habsburg Empress, Maria Theresa) was one of the Hungarian capital's busiest and most densely populated districts.

'Etelka was only 38 years old when she went to look at the apartment,' says my mother. 'But she was in a lot of pain with her swollen legs and there was no lift in the building.'

The resident caretaker, or *házmester*, to whom Etelka introduced herself, took pity on her. He suggested that, in order to form an idea of what the vacant, third floor apartment was like, she could look round his flat instead. He explained that the two apartments were virtually identical except that his flat, which was situated on the ground

The perils of smoking a pipe

The courtyard of an apartment building in Budapest, 1944

floor, was quite a bit darker. Etelka gratefully accepted the *házmester*'s offer. In the end, she moved into the third-floor apartment with her family without having seen it for herself.

'Can you remember the layout of your apartment?'

'The entrance was from one of those internal walkways you often find in older Budapest apartment buildings,' says my mother. 'On one side, they're completely open to the elements with just a railing of some kind for security.' As I knew from personal experience, such walkways can be daunting, particularly for anyone with a fear of heights.

'As you entered the flat you found yourself in a tiny hallway which led directly to the kitchen,' continues my mother. 'From the kitchen, a door opened onto the apartment's only room.'

'Wasn't it very cramped? How could you fit all your beds and other furniture into just one room?'

My mother shrugs. 'We managed. My parents slept on two single beds that were pushed together,' she tells me. 'I slept on the sofa, while my brother, Öcsi, had to make do with a collapsible bed that was erected each evening. During the day, it was stored away under my parents' beds.'

'Is that everything?'

'Well, there was a dining table and some chairs, as well as an old wardrobe for our clothes,' adds my mother. 'Etelka was ashamed of the apartment because it was so small and shabby. Very few of her old friends, who'd known her when she lived in the grand apartment on Nagymező *utca*, ever came to visit her. Maybe just one or two.'

'What about the lavatory?'

'The toilet was situated on the communal landing,' recalls my mother. 'We shared the toilet with Karcsi and his two older sisters who occupied the neighbouring apartment. Fortunately, we all got on very well.' Like Etelka and her family, Karcsi and his sisters were Jewish. Originally from Szolnok, a medium-sized provincial town, they'd moved to Budapest in search of work.

'In the evenings, after Öcsi and I had gone to bed, Etelka would spend an hour or more in the kitchen preparing a cooked lunch for Miklós for the following day,' says my mother. 'He would take it with him the next morning and reheat it on a stove at the filling station. Karcsi or one of his sisters would often come over and chat with Etelka while she cooked.'

'What about washing? How did you manage to keep clean without a bath or a shower?'

My mother smiles. 'We had a hip bath which was hung on a nail in the kitchen. A couple of times a week my mother would take it down and fill it with water that she'd heated on the stove. We took turns in the bath. We children always washed first.'

'You all bathed in the same water?'

'Of course!' exclaims my mother, laughing. 'Heating enough water for the hip bath took a lot of time and effort!'

Coal or firewood had to be fetched for the stove, which meant descending four flights of stairs to the cellar where each flat had its own bunker. Carrying two heavy pails, filled to the brim with coal, Etelka often struggled when coming back up.

'She refused to let Miklós help her,' says my mother. 'Etelka could see that he was exhausted by the time he came home. Fortunately, the swelling and pain in her legs had eased now that she no longer worked at the *kifőzde*.'

My mother pauses, lost in thought. 'Years ago, when Öcsi and I spent a few days together in London, I asked him if he remembered how Miklós got to work?' she continues. 'Miklós had to be at the filling station in Csepel by 4:30 a.m. on weekdays, well before trams or buses were even running.'

This conversation between Öcsi and my mother took place late one night while the two of them were staying in Etelka's studio apartment in Bloomsbury. Brother and sister, now middle-aged and settled in Canada and the Netherlands respectively, had been reunited in London after Etelka had been rushed to hospital with suspected kidney failure. In a reversion to their Budapest childhood, Öcsi and my mother slept in the same room once more, the only room in Etelka's tiny flat, spending their days at Etelka's bedside in the hospital. Etelka was to die a few days afterwards.

'Öcsi's memory was always much better than mine,' says my mother. 'He remembered that, on weekdays, Miklós would get up at 3:00 a.m. Once he was washed and dressed and had had something to eat, he'd make his way on foot to the *Oktogon*, walking very slowly because of his bad leg.'

At the *Oktogon*, one of the busiest intersections in downtown Budapest, Miklós would hail a passing horse and cart bound for Csepel's wholesale food market. Miklós was on friendly terms with many of the carters who went to the market very early each day to collect fruit, vegetables, and other produce for shops across the city. The carters were happy to accept a few coins in return for giving my grandfather a lift and were glad of the company.

'It must have been pretty miserable for him in the depths of winter,' muses my mother. 'Sitting up there on a cart, with no protection from the elements.' Like its people and its politics, Hungary's central continental climate is prone to extremes. At least until the onset of global warming, winters were almost always long and bitter, with icy roads, heavy snowfalls, and rivers and lakes that were frozen over for weeks or even months at a time.

'Why didn't he hitch a ride with one of the trucks taking produce to the market? At least it would have been warm in the cab and he wouldn't have got soaked if it rained.'

'I don't know,' says my mother. 'I think truck drivers delivering produce to the market in Csepel generally took a different route. Or maybe they would have asked for more money?'

A biplane manufactured by the Manfréd Weiss
Steel and Metal Works, 1940

Miklós wouldn't recognize Csepel now. In the 1930s and early 1940s, when my grandfather worked at the filling station next to the wholesale food market, some of Hungary's most important industries were located in Csepel, a natural island bounded by two rivers. In 1892, the brothers Manfréd and Bertold Weiss moved their munitions factory to Csepel after an accidental explosion at their plant in Budapest's Ninth District. In the years that followed, Manfréd expanded the business until it became the largest and most important industrial concern in the Hungarian sector of the Austro-Hungarian Empire. By the eve of World War Two, the Manfréd Weiss Steel and Metal Works, as it came to be known, employed 40,000 people and manufactured everything from munitions to motor cars, from aeroplanes to bicycles.[42]

Following World War Two, Csepel was gradually transformed. Many of the factories closed, while hundreds of utilitarian apartment buildings were built to ease Budapest's acute post-War housing shortage. The wholesale food market was relocated elsewhere.

'Miklós left the filling station at three in the afternoon,' says my mother, resuming her narrative. 'But that still wasn't the end of his working day. After locking up he had to bring the day's takings to the Company's offices in Budapest.'

On one occasion, recalls my mother, Miklós, a pipe smoker, had his pipe in his mouth when he knocked and entered his line manager's office. 'The man was absolutely furious! He sprang to his feet and knocked the pipe out of my father's mouth!' says my mother, indignantly. 'What do you mean by talking to me with a pipe in your mouth?' the manager had demanded.

'How did your father react? Was he angry or upset?'

'No, not really,' says my mother. 'He just told us about the incident. He seemed to take it all quite philosophically.'

Unlike many adults, whose parenting skills bring to mind the immortal lines of Philip Larkin — 'They fuck you up, your mum and dad/ They may not mean to, but they do'[43] — Miklós doesn't seem to have instilled any neuroses or inhibitions in his children. He wasn't sarcastic or patronising, and he never made unreasonable demands of them. 'Miklós never shouted at me or my brother, and he never once raised his hand to either of us,' recalls my mother. As a father, his love was abundant, uncomplicated, and unconditional.

Yet, in another and perhaps equally important sense, Miklós was a failure, both as a parent and as a husband. From the day he married Etelka, in August 1924, until the moment he was hustled away by *Nyilas* militiamen, almost exactly twenty years later, Miklós rarely earned enough money to look after his family properly. Again and again in my mother's stories about her childhood, a childhood that she always insists was extremely happy, I am conscious of the fact that her early years were shaped by the family's chronic poverty.

Unlike Dr. Zsigmond Hegyi and his wife Bianka, who lived in a spacious, comfortable apartment in the upmarket Újlipotváros district of the city, Miklós could barely afford the rent on the gloomy little flat on Szinyei Merse *utca*. As a teenager, my mother continued to share the apartment's only room with her parents and younger brother.

The lack of a nutritious, varied diet, a direct consequence of the family's meagre income, almost certainly accounted for many of their health problems. 'From time to time, my father developed boils on his neck and back,' recalls my mother. 'He'd have to go to one of the clinics run by the OTI and have them lanced.' The OTI, or *Országos Társadalombistositási Intézet*, was a national insurance scheme, established in Hungary in the late 1920s to provide modest benefits, including medical care, for workers.[44]

Ensuring that her children were properly clothed became a source of endless worry for Etelka. 'As a child, Öcsi had to undergo a minor operation,' says my mother. Ashamed that he didn't have a decent pair of pyjamas that he could wear while he was an inpatient in the hospital — Öcsi's only pyjamas were heavily patched — Etelka borrowed a pair from an old schoolfriend who had a son about Öcsi's age.

'Mr. Seres, the shoesmith, had his basement workshop directly across the road from us,' says my mother. 'If I or my brother took our shoes to him he had to repair them right away. We only had a single pair each. It was exactly the same for our parents.'

Even in old age my mother recalls the humiliation she felt at her high-school graduation ceremony. Walking to the front of the packed auditorium to receive her *érettségi*, my mother was acutely conscious of not being properly dressed. 'It was customary for all the girls who were graduating to wear a dark skirt and a *matrózblúz* or white sailor's blouse with a pretty blue collar,' says my mother. 'Anyone could see that mine wasn't a proper *matrózblúz*.' To economise, Etelka had bought a cheap blue collar which she'd sewn inexpertly onto an ordinary — and far from new — white blouse.

'Etelka tried to earn a little extra money to supplement Miklós' wages,' says my mother. 'She sold advertising space for a local newspaper on a commission basis. She also offered to do grocery shopping for her old friends.'

'Wasn't that humiliating for Etelka, as well as embarrassing for her friends?'

'I suppose it must have been,' my mother says.

'Once he was old enough, Öcsi would go off most Sundays with his scout troop,' says my mother. 'Etelka usually stayed at home to get on with the housework. Very occasionally, we'd all go for a hike in the Buda hills with Aunt Klára and her family.'

On those Sundays when Öcsi was with his scout troop and Etelka was preoccupied with domestic chores, Miklós liked to visit one of his brothers or sisters, most of whom lived in or near Budapest. Etelka had no objection, provided my mother accompanied him.

'Etelka was neurotically jealous,' says my mother, who only came to understand Etelka's motives and character many years afterwards. 'She had somehow convinced herself that Miklós would cheat on her if he had the slightest chance.'

Perhaps it was my grandfather's fastidiousness about his personal appearance that aroused Etelka's suspicions? On Sunday mornings, before setting off to call on one of his relatives, Miklós would polish his shoes and carefully brush his suit, all the while humming a popular tune. Miklós always checked in the mirror that his moustache was neatly trimmed and that his soft, limp hair was properly combed. In her heavily Hungarian-accented English, my mother says that Miklós looked 'teeptawp'.

Etelka's sexual jealousy may also have stemmed from deep-seated feelings of insecurity. My grandmother never truly believed that she was attractive enough to retain the interest of a man who was three years younger than her and whom she considered extremely handsome, despite his disability. Budapest's well-deserved reputation for loose morals may also have played a part in fuelling my grandmother's anxieties, which spread cancer-like through her marriage, each malignant cell of suspicion dividing and multiplying over time.

With his high, domed forehead and sharp angular features culminating in a narrow chin, Miklós may not have been blessed with the classic good looks of a George Clooney or a Brad Pitt. But Miklós remained slim, even in middle age, and he was handsome enough, even if he lacked the sexually charged chemistry of a Humphrey Bogart or a young Marlon Brando. Etelka was determined not to give her husband the slightest opportunity to stray.

'On Sundays, my father and I often went to visit Aunt Klára and Uncle Imre who lived in Buda with their son Gyuri,' says my mother. As mentioned earlier, Klára suffered from tuberculosis. Her husband supported the family entirely from his modest earnings as a shop assistant.

'Sometimes we'd pay a call on Uncle Marci,' recalls my mother. 'Compared with the rest of us, Marci was very well off. He and his family lived in a comfortable rented apartment in Buda.'

Marci, one of my grandfather's younger brothers, had been an indifferent pupil at school. Unlike Miklós, he didn't even sit his *érettségi*. However, once he left school, Marci, who had a good head for business and a confident, agreeable manner, quickly showed himself to be able and ambitious. After starting out as a sales assistant in a shop selling textiles, Marci worked his way up to become the Budapest representative of a large textile company based in Pécs, an important city in the south of Hungary.

Miklós' other brother Jenő, whom he often visited on Sundays accompanied by my mother, possessed none of the dynamism or ambition displayed by Marci or, in his younger days, by their father. Jenő, who qualified as a printer, had married a devout peasant woman and converted to the Catholic faith for the sake of his wife.[45] The couple and their children lived in a simple, one-room house in Pesterzsébet. Now a suburb of Budapest, Pesterzsébet was then a rapidly expanding town. Despite its size and proximity to the capital — by 1930, its population had swelled to 67,000 — Pesterzsébet remained provincial and underdeveloped.

'The roads weren't paved!' recalls my mother, with horror. 'Depending on the season, we might have to walk in thick mud all the way from the tram stop to Uncle Jenő's house!' Her uncle's modest dwelling was built entirely from cob; the toilet was an earth closet at the bottom of the garden.

'Miklós would always take his brother and sister-in-law a present, perhaps a watermelon or a chicken,' continues my mother. 'We would eat Sunday lunch together, which was usually *nyúlpörkölt* or some other dish featuring rabbit. In those days, rabbit was far and away the cheapest meat you could buy.'

My mother recalls that these Sunday visits to Uncle Jenő and Aunt Margit, who were straightforward and kindly, always passed off agreeably. My mother got on particularly well with Jenő and Margit's children, two boys and a girl, who were close enough to her in age. However, within the space of a few years, relations with Tibi, one of her cousins, had deteriorated alarmingly.

—⁂—

'Tibi strode into our apartment in Szinyei Merse *utca*,' says my uncle, when I interviewed him at his suburban home in Toronto. It is late spring 1944 and German forces have occupied Hungary. Budapest's Jews have been ordered to vacate their homes and to move into newly designated 'star houses' located at various points around the city.[46] The buildings took their name from the yellow Star of David on a black background displayed by their entrances.[47]

'Tibi stood in the middle of our one-room apartment, carefully appraising our possessions,' says my uncle. 'He pointed at a couple of pieces of furniture and calmly told us, "I'm going to take these for myself!"' Miklós and Etelka had stared at their nephew helplessly.

'I don't understand,' I tell my uncle. 'I know Tibi was born a Catholic and that his father had converted to the Catholic faith when he married Margit. Even so, wasn't Tibi classified as a Jew under Hungary's anti-Jewish laws?' Hungary enacted a series of increasingly draconian anti-Jewish laws, beginning in 1938.[48]

My uncle shakes his head. 'I don't know how he managed it but Tibi joined the *Nyilas*, the Hungarian Nazis, when he was still in his teens. He really hated Jews, even though he was half-Jewish himself.'

It's only later that I obtain copies of Hungary's Jewish laws, passed in a climate of sharply escalating anti-Semitism and at a time when Hungary was forging an increasingly close alliance with Nazi Germany. According to the Second Jewish Law, which entered into force in May 1939, the statute did not apply to anyone, like Tibi, whose parents, 'had been members of a Christian denomination at the time of their marriage and had remained members of a Christian denomination since that time'.[49]

Aunt Margit's fervent religiosity and, in particular, her unquestioning adherence to the dogmas of the Catholic Church had saved her children from the potentially fatal misfortune of being classified as Jews. By insisting on Jenő's conversion to the Catholic faith *before* their marriage — and by ensuring that their children were baptised and raised as observant members of the Church — she had unknowingly protected them from the fate that befell their Jewish cousins.

Although uncompromising in matters of religion, Aunt Margit was said to have been extremely warm and generous in her dealings with others, particularly members of the family. Far from shunning her husband's Jewish relatives, she welcomed them into her home. As mentioned previously, Margit cared for Jenő's elderly parents, Adolf and Teréz, after Teréz fell ill with cancer. However, despite her admirable personal qualities, Margit failed to instil a sense of compassion or human decency in one of her children, Tibi.

'Tibi disappeared towards the end of the War,' says my uncle. 'His parents heard that he'd been captured by a Red Army unit not long after the Soviets succeeded in taking Budapest.' Able-bodied and in his late teens, the Soviets would have assumed that Tibi had taken an active part in the defence of the capital, together with tens of thousands of German and Hungarian troops, *Nyilas* militiamen, gendarmes, students and others.

'After they'd finished interrogating him, the Soviets executed Tibi,' says my uncle. 'At least, that's what his parents were told.'

Like his Soviet interrogators, I can't help wondering what Tibi may have done after the *Nyilas* Party seized power, in October 1944, with the assistance of Nazi Germany.[50] And how had Tibi conducted himself during the protracted siege of Budapest? As a *Nyilas* militiaman, perhaps Tibi fought bravely alongside German and Hungarian troops against the encroaching Soviet forces? Maybe Tibi was commended by his commanding officer for conspicuous acts of valour?

However, knowing something of his character and political inclinations, it seems far more likely that Tibi was complicit in atrocities against Jewish civilians and other supposed enemies of the Hungarian nation. Maybe Tibi helped to slaughter Jews, including women and children, on the banks of the Danube in the winter of 1944-45, casually shoving the corpses into the freezing water? Perhaps Tibi participated in the drunken, murderous raids on Budapest's Jewish ghetto? Or maybe he was involved in the notorious 'death marches' in late 1944, helping to escort some of the tens of thousands of Jewish men and women who made the week-long journey on foot, from Budapest to the border, without adequate food, water, shelter, or medical care?[51] Perhaps it's wrong of me to feel this way, but I wouldn't be unduly sorry to learn that Soviet interrogators hadn't been gentle with Tibi, before finally despatching him with a single bullet to the back of the head. Unlike his mild-mannered father, his devout mother or his artistic brother Bandi — who subsequently made a new life for himself in Paris — Tibi had shown a natural affinity with the thuggery, rampant opportunism and murderous anti-Semitism of the *Nyilaskeresztes* Party.

13

The meaning of chocolate

In a short story by Dezső Kosztolányi, published in 1930, a middle-aged Hungarian schoolmaster enjoys a month-long summer vacation at a spa in the Austrian hills. Kosztolányi, who was one of Hungary's most celebrated poets as well as a prolific and talented prose writer, sums up the bracing micro-climate of the region in a single sentence: 'rain smelling of salt and resin fell in the mornings, by noon bright sunshine pierced the dense wall of pine trees, the afternoon was scorchingly hot, the evening wintry'.[52]

Dezső Kosztolányi, 1935

The schoolmaster, a confirmed bachelor, is far from affluent and has to budget carefully. At the end of his vacation he returns home to Hungary in 'a crowded second-class railway compartment' rather than travelling in comfort in first class or in a motor car. The purchase of a three-piece suit, which the schoolmaster mistakenly believes he has ordered from a tailor recommended to him by a former pupil, constitutes a major investment requiring careful deliberation. In Budapest, the schoolmaster habitually has his solitary supper in a modest inn, allowing himself just a single glass of red wine. Yet, despite his limited means and frugal lifestyle, the schoolmaster can afford a month-long summer vacation in an Austrian spa, taking his meals in the dining room of the spa's hotel.

Like his fictional creation, Kosztolányi enjoyed foreign travel while, unlike the cautious and parsimonious schoolmaster, he had the means to travel widely and often. We know from Kosztolányi's articles, written for various newspapers and subsequently published as a book, that he visited Rome, Paris, London, Berlin, and Vienna.[53] He also recorded his impressions of Belgrade, Venice, Grenoble, Oxford, Dover, Munich, Strasbourg, Malmö, Stockholm, Würzburg, and Amsterdam. Kosztolányi once wrote that he was fascinated by everything that he encountered abroad, no matter how trivial, including the chime of a doorbell and the shape of a window. In another piece, originally published in *Pesti Hírlap* in October 1924, Kosztolányi confessed that he liked foreign travel first and foremost because it afforded him the possibility of anonymity and of personal renewal: 'people don't know me… everything can begin afresh'.[54]

A generation earlier, the 'nation's nightingale' Lujza Blaha liked to spend the summer months quietly, with family and friends, in Balatonfüred. Blaha, who acquired a handsome villa in the elegant Hungarian spa town, records the events of a typical summer's day in her diary.[55] In fine weather, she would rise at five thirty in the morning to take a long and frequently solitary walk in woodland or by the

My mother in Balatonfüred, 1941

lake. On her way back, she would pause to pray at a church before taking breakfast at home with her family.

The remainder of the morning was frequently given over to bathing in the lake while, at noon, accompanied by her husband or other companions, she would stroll down to the pier to see if she recognised any of the passengers arriving that day on the steamship. After lunch, the actress generally took a nap before setting out on yet another walk. In the evenings, weather permitting, supper was taken out of doors. Lujza Blaha liked to be in bed no later than nine thirty. This unvarying regime, centred on rest, gentle exercise, and regular, nourishing meals, helped her to recoup her energies for the rigours of the impending theatrical season.

'We never took holidays as a family,' says my mother. 'There was never enough money.' For Miklós and Etelka, family holidays, no matter how short or inexpensive, represented an unimaginable luxury. So my mother was thrilled when, at the age of twelve or thirteen, she was invited by her uncle and aunt to spend a couple of weeks with them in Balaton-füred during the summer. This was to be the first of several working holidays that my mother spent with Tódor and Ilona in the lakeside resort.

As previously mentioned, Tódor and Ilona ran a small giftshop attached to one of the spa town's oldest and most venerable hotels. The little shop, which was located on the ground floor of the hotel, was all that remained of the 'business empire' that Adolf Faragó, Ilona's energetic, entrepreneurial but serially unlucky father once dreamed of bequeathing to his children. The printing works, the local newspaper and the open-air cinema that Adolf is said to have founded, after moving to Balatonfüred sometime before World War One, had long since closed or been sold off.

A number of things are immediately apparent from the photograph of my mother taken in Balatonfüred in the summer of 1941. Perhaps most strikingly, my mother is drably and soberly dressed although it's the height of summer. Standing by the edge of the lake, a couple of yachts just visible in the background, my mother is wearing what must have been an uncomfortably dark skirt, a white top that reaches primly to her neck, and white, open-topped shoes. The voluminous shopping bag that my mother is holding in her left hand suggests that the photograph was taken while she was running an errand for her uncle and aunt. However, it's clear from my mother's open, unaffected smile that she's enjoying herself.

My mother's abundant curly hair, so carefully coiffed in adulthood, is sticking out in all directions. Ever since the death of Aunt Ilus, a professional hairdresser who had her own salon in Budapest, my mother has been forced to rely on the services of Etelka, whose inept and impatient efforts with scissors and comb left a great deal to be desired.

'The first time Ilona invited me to stay with them I assumed it was for a holiday,' says my mother, laughing. 'I was so excited; I'd never been to Lake Balaton. I could hardly wait to see the lake and to go for a swim! It was only after I arrived that Ilona and Tódor explained that they expected me to work in their shop.'

It's a bright sunny day in late spring as my mother and I slowly make our way through a beautifully tended park towards Balatonfüred's famous sanatorium. As in the 1920s, when Rabindranath Tagore was a patient here, the hospital specialises in the treatment of ailments of the heart. According to my mother, Tódor and Ilona's shop, selling everything from postcards and souvenirs to shoelaces, swimming caps, and beach towels, was located in the lobby of a hotel located directly opposite the sanatorium.

'Do you remember the name of the hotel?' I ask. It's June 2016. In a few weeks' time, my mother will celebrate her ninetieth birthday. She last visited her uncle and aunt in Balatonfüred as a teenager.

'I think it was called the Savoy,' says my mother, uncertainly. 'No,' she corrects herself, 'it was called the Stefánia'.

By 1911, there were already several hotels and pensions in Balatonfüred, catering to a variety of tastes and budgets. They included Horváth House, the Hotel Eszterházy, the Grand Hotel, Erzsébet Court, Klotild Court, and Ipoly Court. By the eve of World War One, as the number of visitors to the town continued to grow, they were augmented by the Annuska Pension, Terézia Court, and the Dőry Villa.

Horváth House, originally built in the eighteenth century directly across from the sanatorium, has been known by various names and has had a number of different functions. In many respects, Horváth House serves as an apt metaphor for Hungary, mirroring the brusque and sometimes brutal changes that the country has undergone. During the nineteenth century, at a time of growing national pride and self-confidence, Horváth House hosted many of the country's leading public figures, including the great economic and cultural reformer Count István Széchenyi and the revered elder statesman Ferenc Deák.[56] The latter is said to have spent as much as four or five weeks in Balatonfüred each summer, which had grown into the largest and most fashionable resort on the lake. The presence of men such as Széchenyi and Deák, as well as of eminent writers and poets, attracted a host of mostly younger admirers, eager to catch a glimpse of their heroes and to sample some of the diversions that Balatonfüred and the surrounding area had to offer.

Following World War One, as the country confronted the twin traumas of defeat and dismemberment, Horváth House fell into disrepair. By the end of World War Two, in which Hungary once again managed to pick the losing side — fatally allying itself with Hitler and Nazi Germany — Horváth House was transformed into a hospital and convalescent home for members of Hungary's armed forces. From the early 1950s, as Soviet-style Communism was introduced in Hungary, Horváth House was proletarianized. Having played host to aristocrats, statesmen, and prominent literary figures, it now provided heavily subsidised holidays for miners and other employees of the state-owned Mecseki Uranium Ore Company, together with their families.[57]

Today, in the second decade of the twenty-first century, Horváth House caters to an altogether different clientele. As in the eighteenth and nineteenth centuries, Horváth House is patronised by wealthy and discerning guests, although there aren't many aristocrats or statesmen amongst them.

Balatonfüred, 1934

In present-day Hungary there are few, if any, public figures of the calibre of Széchenyi or Deák — men of vision, unshakeable moral purpose and unwavering commitment to the national interest. In place of the old aristocracy, with their elegant manners, archaic titles, and draughty palaces, a new, monied 'aristocracy', with its political connections, has risen up in its place.

In keeping with the requirements of high-end modern tourism, Horváth House offers tastefully furnished holiday apartments situated on the upper floors of the building, while an imposing restaurant and wine cellar can be found below. The restaurant's menu boasts that the establishment offers 'culinary art of the highest quality', a claim that is amply reflected in its prices.

Since it was founded, Horváth House has undergone various changes of nomenclature. Following the acquisition of the building in 1878 by a local physician, Dr. Henrik Mangold, the hotel was rechristened Mangold House. However, for much of the inter-war period, including the years in which my mother visited Balatonfüred each summer for a working holiday, it was known as Stefánia *Udvar* or Stefánia Court.

'Uncle Tódor would put on his swimming trunks every day, in the early afternoon, and leave the shop for an hour or so to swim in the lake,' recalls my mother, with a chuckle. 'He never invited me to accompany him. I was expected to stay in the shop, with Aunt Ilona, helping to serve the customers.'

My mother laughs at the recollection of Tódor's self-centredness although, at the time, it must have been disheartening to have to watch her uncle saunter out of the hot, stuffy shop and to know that, within minutes, he'd be immersed in the cooling waters of the lake. 'Just once,' says my mother, 'Uncle Tódor remained in the shop and told me that I could go for a swim instead.'

Amongst my carefully hoarded collection of family photographs there are two of my mother taken at Balaton-füred. In one, which features on the cover of this book, my mother is barely more than a child. In the other, repro-duced above, she is a slightly awkward-looking teenager. But I have no photographs of Aunt Ilona or of Uncle Tódor.

'What did your aunt and uncle look like?'

My mother struggles to describe Tódor, who would have been in his early forties, like his wife, when my mother first went to stay with them. According to my mother, Tódor was neither thin nor fat, neither short nor tall. He wasn't particularly handsome but neither was he ugly.

'Did Tódor have a beard or a moustache?'

'No', says my mother. 'Uncle Tódor was cleanshaven'.

'Was he bald?'

'No, he had a pretty full head of hair.'

By contrast, my mother has no difficulty in describing Ilona, who was one of her father's younger sisters. 'Aunt

Ilona was extremely tall and very thin,' says my mother. 'She wasn't remotely sexy.'

Fortunately, Uncle Tódor seems to have had a more favourable opinion of his wife. 'Sometimes, in the evenings, Uncle Tódor would ask my aunt for a piece of chocolate,' recalls my mother. 'I soon came to understand what that meant.' In the couple's private but easily breakable code, chocolate signified sex. If Aunt Ilona gave her husband a piece of chocolate it meant that she consented to his request for conjugal relations.

'They were always very quiet about it,' says my mother, who slept in the same room as her uncle and aunt. 'But I realised what was going on, even though I never heard panting or anything of that sort.'

Up to this point I had always assumed that Tódor and Ilona, who were childless, lived in a comfortable, rented apartment in Balatonfüred, or maybe in a house. In reality, says my mother, the couple lived in a single room directly behind their shop: 'Uncle Tódor and Aunt Ilona slept in a double bed. I slept in a bed near the door, in the corner.'

Although the couple's living quarters could hardly be described as spacious, let alone luxurious, Ilona and Tódor enjoyed a far higher standard of living than my mother was accustomed to in Budapest. 'My uncle and aunt ordered in really tasty cooked meals every day!' says my mother, almost in wonder. 'Aunt Ilona worked all day in the shop, which was often quite busy. She didn't have time to buy food or to cook. The shop stayed open as long as there were customers.'

'Did they pay you a wage or give you pocket money?'

'No, there was never any question of that,' says my mother. 'Actually, now I think about it, they never even gave me a present. Not even something from their shop.'

Yet my mother harbours no resentment towards her uncle and aunt. 'They were always very kind to me,' she says, firmly. For my mother, who had hardly ever travelled outside Budapest, these annual working holidays in Balatonfüred represented a welcome break, although she readily admits that she would have liked to go swimming more often and to have had an opportunity to make friends with people of her own age.

'Once my uncle and aunt took me with them on an excursion to Tihany, a local beauty spot,' says my mother. On that memorable day the shop, which was usually open all through the week during the busy summer months, remained shuttered and closed.

Just a few kilometres from Balatonfüred, the Tihany peninsula is easily accessible by bus or passenger ferry as well as by motorcar. Rising to a height of 235 metres, Tihany offers unrivalled views over the Balaton. With its panoramic vistas and ancient Benedictine Abbey, Tihany was already a popular tourist destination in the 1930s.

'We had lunch outside, in the garden of a little family-run *vendéglő*,' recalls my mother, who had never eaten a meal in a restaurant with her parents. For Etelka and Miklós, thriftiness, the unceasing need to guard against the slightest unnecessary expenditure, overshadowed their adult lives. But my mother's delight at finally finding herself in a restaurant, however modest, was marred by the diminutive size of the portions.

'We all had *pörkölt*, a kind of stew seasoned with paprika. It was delicious but it was served on very small plates,' explains my mother. 'That was the custom in those days. People ate their main meal in the evening.'

Perhaps my mother is right. Maybe portions, particularly at luncheon, were smaller when she was a teenager. However, I can't help wondering whether Tódor and Ilona ordered *zóna* or half-portions to economise.[58] Although their little shop did reasonably well during the summer months, the couple were far from rich. And, with anti-Semitism rapidly gaining ground in Hungary — Hungary's First Anti-Jewish Law had been adopted in 1938 — Tódor and Ilona may have thought it prudent to build up their savings. Who knew when they might need them?

'The last time I went to stay with Uncle Tódor and Aunt Ilona was in 1941,' says my mother. She doesn't know why these annual working holidays came to an abrupt end. 'I got on really well with both my uncle and aunt. I always tried to do everything I could to please them.'

Perhaps Tódor and Ilona felt that my mother was no longer a child and that it would be inappropriate for her to go on sharing a room with them? Maybe Aunt Ilona, aging, unfeminine, and painfully gaunt, was worried that Tódor had a roving eye? Perhaps she was concerned that my mother's youth and increasingly womanly figure would present too much of a temptation for her husband?

It's conceivable that there was so much to do in the shop, particularly in the summer months, that the couple had decided to hire local help, someone who could work for them for the entire holiday season. However, it's far more likely that trade had fallen off, which would have meant that Uncle Tódor and Aunt Ilona no longer needed my mother's services. As the campaign against 'Jewish influence' in Hungary's economy and cultural life reached unprecedented heights — and as the government forged an increasingly close alliance with Nazi Germany — many Jewish-owned stores suffered a severe loss of business. In towns and villages across Hungary, Jewish shopkeepers had been forced to display notices alerting customers to the fact that the premises were Jewish-owned.[59] In some parts of the country, gentile shopkeepers were encouraged to put up signs stating that their businesses belonged to Christians.

'What happened to your uncle and aunt?' I ask my mother. 'When did you see them next?'

My mother stares at me blankly. 'I never saw Tódor or Ilona ever again,' she replies, matter of factly. Despite persistent efforts after World War Two, Etelka was unable to discover anything about the couple's fate.

Records show that 153 Jews were transported from Balatonfüred on 15 May 1944, arriving in Auschwitz-Birkenau several weeks later.[60] In the intervening period, they were held in makeshift ghettos, initially in Tapolca and subsequently in the town of Zalaegerszeg. The horrific conditions in the Zalaegerszeg ghetto prompted several Jews to commit suicide, while others were murdered by the Hungarian gendarmes assigned to guard them.[61]

After the end of hostilities, only fifteen Jews returned to Balatonfüred.[62] This figure includes several Jewish men from the town who'd been conscripted into auxiliary labour battalions, as well as Jews who'd survived Auschwitz. Neither Tódor nor Ilona was amongst them.

14
Good times

'When was this taken?' I ask my mother, holding up a small, black and white photograph, one of a pile that lie strewn across my dining table. Despite an interval of over seventy years my mother is instantly recognizable. She is standing between a cheerful, smiling girl in a skirt and blouse and a tall, well-built youth dressed in a jacket and plus fours.

As the family's self-appointed historian, I have greedily accumulated all the photos and documents that I can. Although most of my family's possessions were lost in the upheavals and dislocation of World War Two — or abandoned when they left Hungary after the 1956 Revolution

— I have collected enough materials to fill a medium-sized briefcase.

'That photograph was taken in spring 1943,' says my mother, without a moment's hesitation.

Are you sure? Perhaps it was earlier?'

'It was 1943. I'm quite certain,' replies my mother, testily. Although this conversation took place when my mother was already in her ninety-first year, she had lost little, if any, of her mental acuity. Happily settled in the Netherlands since the late 1960s, my mother continued to play bridge twice a week, gave English conversation classes to a group of elderly Dutch ladies, and cruised the Dutch waterways with my father each summer in a handsome old river boat that they purchased when they were already in their seventies.

I struggle to digest what my mother has just told me. At the height of World War Two, when Hitler and Nazi Germany controlled most of mainland Europe, my mother and her Jewish friends were enjoying a pleasant hike in the Buda hills. From their smiling faces and relaxed demeanour you'd think that these young people didn't have a care in the world. 'We used to meet regularly on Sundays to go walking,' my mother says.

By the time that this photograph was taken, the genocide of Europe's Jews was well underway, although my mother and her companions were unaware of it. Following Germany's invasion of the Soviet Union, in June 1941, Jews were methodically slaughtered by German *Einsatzgruppen* in territories newly occupied by the *Wehrmacht*.[63] Chelmno, the first dedicated extermination facility, was opened in December of that year, while Belżec and Auschwitz-Birkenau were functioning by March 1942.[64] Sobibór's gas chambers were busy from May of the same year, and Treblinka was fully operational by July.[65]

In the summer of 1941, a couple of years before this photograph of my mother and her friends was taken, peasants and townsfolk in the Polish town of Jedwabne butchered and plundered their Jewish neighbours under the benign gaze of the occupying German forces.[66] Several hundred of the town's Jews, including babies and infants, were herded into a wooden barn that was set on fire. Anyone trying to escape the flames was brutally killed. In the Polish capital Warsaw, hundreds of thousands of Jews were confined to an overcrowded, disease-ridden ghetto from which they were sent in batches to Treblinka for extermination.[67]

In July 1942, a full year before this photograph of my mother and her friends was taken in the Buda hills, Irène Némirovsky was arrested in the village of Issy l'Éveque as a 'stateless person of Jewish descent'. An émigrée Russian who was lionized in inter-war France for her novels, written in flawless and elegant French, Némirovsky was initially held in an internment camp at Pithiviers and later transported to Auschwitz along with several hundred other Jews from France.[68] Némirovsky, who had converted to the Catholic faith in 1939, died of typhus a month after entering the camp. In November 1942, Némirovsky's husband, unaware of the fate of his wife, was selected for the gas chambers on arrival at Auschwitz-Birkenau. Their young daughters, who had been sent into hiding, survived.[69]

In the Netherlands, which had been a haven for Jews fleeing persecution from as early as the sixteenth century, 107,000 Jews were diligently rounded up by Dutch police between July 1942 and September of the following year and despatched to Auschwitz, Sobibór, and other camps.[70] Scarcely more than 5,000 remained alive at the end of the War.

In the midst of the unprecedented genocide of Europe's Jews, how had my mother and her Jewish friends managed to avoid a similar fate? How were they able to lead apparently normal lives as late as spring or even autumn 1943?

Although they were unaware of it, my mother and her companions owed their relative, if merely temporary, good fortune to Hungary's alliance with Nazi Germany. Hungarian troops had participated in the Axis campaign against Yugoslavia, beginning in April 1941, as well as in the ill-fated invasion of the Soviet Union in June of the same year. Throughout 1942 and 1943, Germany continued to treat Hungary as an ally, albeit an increasingly wayward one. German forces did not encroach on Hungarian territory, and the government in Budapest remained fully in Hungarian hands.

Even so, there was mounting impatience in Berlin with Hungary's supposedly lenient treatment of its Jews. At a tense meeting between Hitler and Hungary's Regent, Admiral Horthy, at Klessheim Palace in April 1943, the *Führer* lectured Horthy on the urgent need to take more radical steps against Hungary's Jews. Horthy responded by reminding the *Führer* that Hungary had already taken every conceivable measure against the country's Jews 'that can be decently adopted' and that 'murdering them or eliminating them by other means was hardly possible'.[71]

If Horthy and his Prime Minister Miklós Kállay lacked the genocidal ambition of Hitler and his associates in Berlin, they displayed few qualms about passing sweeping Anti-Jewish Laws. Jewish manual workers employed in privately-owned businesses, like my grandfather, were largely unaffected. By contrast, legislation enacted by Hungary's Parliament in 1939 had envisaged the dismissal or compulsory retirement of *every* Jew employed in the public sector, including teachers in secondary schools.[72] The 1939 law had also suspended the admission of Jews to the liberal professions and to various other occupations in which Jews were heavily represented. The same statute imposed stringent limits on the numbers of Jewish white-collar workers who could be employed by private companies and introduced tough restrictions on Jewish merchants and artisans.

In practice, implementation of the 1939 law proved patchy. As Horthy acknowledged in a letter to Hungary's then Prime Minister Pál Teleki in October 1940, full and prompt application of the anti-Jewish legislation would prove disastrous for the country: 'it is impossible to discard the Jews… in one or two years… because we could flounder. Such a project requires at least one full generation'.[73] Yet, according to the historian Randolph Braham, even partial implementation of the Anti-Jewish Laws, in conjunction with associated legislation, 'had a devastating effect on the economic well-being' of Hungary's Jews.[74]

The smiling and apparently carefree teenagers in the photograph were not immune. Like my mother, then aged seventeen, her companions on that Sunday hike in the Buda hills were mostly still at school, working towards their *érettségi*. They would have known that, however hard they studied, they had little or no chance of obtaining a place at university, of joining one of the professions, or of becoming an actor or journalist. By 1943, even taking up a trade, finding office work, or pursuing a career in commerce was fraught with difficulties for Hungary's Jews, dependent on the whims of employers and bureaucrats and on the administration's shifting perception of its needs.[75] Although the young people in the photograph are smiling, enjoying the warm weather and one another's company, they would have been keenly aware that they faced a range of obstacles that none of their non-Jewish peers had to contend with.

'Zoli was a couple of years older than the rest of us,' says my mother, referring to the athletic-looking young man in plus fours who is standing beside her in the photograph. 'As a Jew there was no way he could have obtained a place at university. He moved to Budapest instead and found a job as a machine-operator in a printing works.'

My mother was introduced to Zoli on one of these weekend rambles in the Budapest hills; she says that they fell in love almost immediately. Zoli, who was something of a ladies' man, had been dating one of the other girls in the photograph when he met my mother. Zoli's jilted girlfriend, who is standing between two female companions, can barely manage a smile for the photographer. She stopped attending the Sunday hikes shortly afterwards.

Zoli — whose full name was Zoltán Füredi — had grown up in Nové Zámky, a small town in southeast Czechoslovakia, where his parents owned a shop. Until the peace settlement following World War One, Nové Zámky had been part of Hungary and was widely known by its Hungarian name, Érsekújvár. As in other towns in what is now southern Slovakia, a sizeable proportion of Érsekújvár's residents, both Christians and Jews, spoke Hungarian as their mother tongue and considered themselves Hungarian in terms of their national identity. Many of them, including Zoli's parents, had opted to remain in Érsekújvár after its inclusion in Czechoslovakia, unwilling or unable to leave their homes and businesses.

In late 1938, Zoli's family suddenly found themselves back in Hungary, without having moved an inch. Following one-sided mediation by Italy and Germany, Czechoslovakia ceded a sizeable strip of territory, including Érsekújvár, to its southern neighbour.[76] However, any pride or satisfaction that Zoli's parents might have felt at this unexpected turn of events would have been tempered by the knowledge that officially sanctioned anti-Semitism had reached unprecedented heights in Hungary, far exceeding anything they had experienced as citizens of Czechoslovakia. Just a few months earlier, Hungary's Parliament had enacted the First Anti-Jewish Law, the 'Law for Assuring More Effective Balance in Social and Economic Life'.[77]

Despite everything going on around them, Zoli and my mother took little interest in politics. They were a young couple and in love. 'I was still at secondary school and I had a lot of studying to do for my *érettségi*,' recalls my mother. 'Zoli wanted us to have more time together so he offered to read some of the Hungarian novels I had to study and to make notes on them.' Relying on Zoli's thorough notes, my mother was able to bypass the time-consuming business of reading some of the classics of Hungarian literature.

As their relationship grew more serious, Zoli and my mother began to plan a married life together, although their romance remained chaste. 'We kissed, nothing more than that,' recalls my mother. 'Zoli told me that he respected me and that he didn't expect me to sleep with him until after we were married.' Zoli nevertheless confided to my mother that, as a man, he had physical needs that he satisfied by visiting a 'woman friend' once a week. This revelation, which would cause most modern relationships to founder, seems to have satisfied my mother. She accepted Zoli's unspoken assumption that male sexuality, in its urgency and intensity, is fundamentally different to the sexual desire experienced by 'respectable' young women.

Zoli wrote to his parents in Érsekújvár telling them of his marriage plans. Curious about their prospective daughter-in-law and her family — and no doubt anxious that their only child should not make a terrible mistake that could blight his future happiness — Zoli's parents came to Budapest for a brief visit.

'I don't think Zoli's mother liked me very much,' says my mother. 'One of the first things she said to me was that she'd heard that I was making her poor son work very hard. That he was having to spend his evenings reading Hungarian literature!'

This reproach suggests that Zoli's mother was a stereotypical Jewish matriarch — both pathologically over-protective of her son and dissatisfied with any woman he might wish to marry. The remark also reveals a boorish disregard for books. Zoli's mother evidently considered reading, particularly works of literature, a hardship.

'They were comfortably off,' says my mother, recalling Zoli's parents, a handsome, slightly fleshy couple in their mid-forties, who impressed her with their fashionable, well-cut clothes and their worldly manner. By contrast, my mother's family lived from one meagre pay-cheque to the next.

'It was summer when Zoli's parents came to Budapest,' continues my mother. 'They suggested that we all go to an afternoon tea dance at one of the hotels on the Corso. My mother came with us.'

The Bristol Hotel on Budapest's Corso, 1943

The Corso, in downtown Pest, remains popular up to the present day, particularly with tourists, affording spectacular views of the Danube and of the principal attractions in Buda. Many of the elegant hotels and restaurants that once lined the Corso, such as the Hotel Bristol in the photo above, were destroyed or irreparably damaged in World War Two. As much as twenty per cent of the city's buildings were razed to the ground or rendered uninhabitable in the fighting.

My mother can no longer remember the name of the hotel in which she took tea with Zoli and his parents. However, she distinctly recalls that a smartly dressed waiter brought them dainty sandwiches, delicious little pastries, and lemon tea. While Etelka chatted politely with Zoli's parents, Zoli and my mother took to the dance floor as the house orchestra struck up a waltz.

'Where was your father? Why wasn't he with you?'

My mother doesn't know. Miklós' working day at the filling station in Csepel would normally have ended by mid-afternoon. It's unlikely that his job had prevented him from coming to meet Zoli's parents.

Perhaps the prospect of having to disclose his menial occupation to these strangers, who owned a successful business and enjoyed a comfortable, middle-class lifestyle, made Miklós uncomfortable? Maybe the thought of having to make polite conversation for hours on end was simply unbearable? Or, as I suspect, Etelka may have told Miklós to stay away, afraid that he might say or do something that would shock this conventional, middle-class Jewish couple from the provinces. After all, Miklós made no secret of the fact that he regarded any form of religion, including Judaism, as little more than an irritating irrelevance, while his meagre earnings and low-grade job would almost certainly have dismayed Zoli's parents. Etelka, having willfully and perhaps foolishly ignored her brother's pleas to marry the hunchback doctor, would have seen Zoli as a good 'catch'. She wouldn't have wanted anything, least of all Miklós, to spoil my mother's marriage prospects. Marrying Zoli, who stood to inherit a thriving business in Nové Zámky, would have allowed her daughter to escape the poverty that had blighted Etelka's life with Miklós.

However, any misgivings that Zoli's parents may have had about my mother or her impoverished, downwardly mobile family were quickly overshadowed by other, more pressing concerns. 'Zoli was called up and I didn't see him again until after the War,' says my mother.

Since summer 1941, Jews had not been permitted to bear arms in the Hungarian army. However, Jewish men up to the age of forty-two were conscripted into auxiliary labour battalions, many of which were assigned to military units.[78] Conditions for labour servicemen were often exceptionally harsh; many were treated with deliberate inhumanity. The story of how Zoli survived, of his eventual return to Budapest, and of his interrupted love affair with my mother, is told in the following chapter.

Part Three

The End of History

15

The poet of the camps

Behind me two corpses/ Before me the world', declared Miklós Radnóti, in a poem that he composed at the age of twenty-eight.[1] The two corpses were those of his mother, who died giving birth to him, and that of his stillborn twin brother of whose existence Radnóti only became aware when he was already in his teens. The significance of the poem's title, *Twenty-eight*, lies in the fact that it is both the age at which Radnóti wrote the poem and also the age at which his mother died.

'Your murderer!' cries Radnóti, perhaps a touch melodramatically, gazing forlornly at a framed photograph of his happy, forever young mother. 'Were the two deaths worth it?'

I can't help feeling that, for Radnóti, the question was rhetorical. His extravagant expressions of remorse at his mother's untimely death coexist uneasily with the searing beauty of his language and with the self-absorption that is evident in the final stanza:

> Mother dear, my blood-soaked victim
> I have grown into manhood
> The sun burns intently, blinding me
> Motion to me with your butterfly hands
> That you know things have turned out well
> That your son is not living his life in vain.

By the time Radnóti came to write these verses he was already an acknowledged, if controversial, poet. Having given up a secure and potentially lucrative career in the textile trade alongside his maternal uncle, who had adopted Radnóti after the death of his father, the young poet devoted himself to his art. In his early twenties, Radnóti helped to found an avant-garde journal, *Kortárs*, published several volumes of poems and enrolled at the University of Szeged where he studied French and Hungarian literature.[2] Radnóti eventually graduated from the university with a doctorate, which received the highest possible grade from his examiners, as well as a teaching certificate.[3]

Miklós Radnóti, 1930

Radnóti's occasionally irreverent verses brought him to the attention of the authorities. In 1931, aged just twenty-two, his home was raided by the police and copies of an anthology containing several of his poems were confiscated. A court in Budapest sentenced the young poet to eight days' imprisonment for blasphemy and libel. However, the sentence was suspended following the intercession of one of Radnóti's professors at Szeged University, Sándor Sík. An accomplished poet, a highly respected literary scholar, and a priest of the Piarist Order, Sík's testimony, in which he averred that Radnóti's poems, though 'tasteless and revolting', were in no sense blasphemous, carried considerable weight with the court.[4] One of the poems that led to Radnóti's prosecution is entitled *Arckép* (*Portrait*). Consisting of just five lines, *Arckép*, in which Radnóti compares himself to Christ — without even a hint of irony or embarrassment — suggests that he already had a highly developed sense of self-worth and perhaps even an awareness of his singular destiny:

> I am twenty-two years old. This
> is how Christ must have looked in autumn
> at the same age; he was fair-haired
> and hadn't yet grown a beard;
> girls fantasised about him in their dreams.

Although Radnóti managed to avoid imprisonment for blasphemy, his second brush with the law, which was wholly unconnected with his art, led inexorably to his death in November 1944. In the intervening years he had married his teenage sweetheart Fanni Gyarmati, embarked on a tempestuous love affair with an artist, Judit Beck, and pursued his burgeoning literary career. Prolific as well as gifted, Radnóti quickly established a reputation in Hungary and abroad as a poet and literary translator. Many of his poems from this period, like *Október, délután*, are sensuous celebrations of the passing seasons and of romantic love. 'Fanni is sleeping beside me under the oak', begins the poem. With the tenderness of a lover, Radnóti describes Fanni as she wakes:

> Fanni awakes, her sleepy eyes blue,
> her beautiful hands like the hands of a saint in a holy painting,
> carefully she brushes off the leaves that have fallen on her as she slept
> before tracing my lips with her hand

her fingers resting a while on my teeth
urging me not to speak.

In the last lines of the poem, Radnóti conjures up an exquisite image of a sudden downpour of rain that persists for several days, 'pinning November on us like a black ribbon'.

However, it is the poems that Radnóti wrote in the final years of his life for which he will be chiefly remembered. Instead of romantic love or the timeless beauties of nature, new subjects had come to dominate Radnóti's art as well as his life — the debasement of social and political mores in Hungary and the intensifying vilification and persecution of the country's Jews. Although Radnóti protested in a letter to the Hungarian-Jewish writer and poet Aladár Komlós that he didn't 'feel Jewish',[5] that he hadn't been 'raised in the Jewish faith', and that he regarded himself as 'just a Hungarian poet', Radnóti had been born into a secular Jewish family. Before changing his name to Radnóti in order to facilitate his acceptance as a Hungarian poet, his family name had been Glatter.

Radnóti's clearly defined sense of identity as a Hungarian poet, as a non-Jew, and as a Catholic were to prove irrelevant. Under the Anti-Jewish Laws enacted from 1938 onwards, Radnóti couldn't escape his Jewishness. As someone born to Jewish parents and still nominally affiliated to the 'Jewish confession' — he only converted to the Catholic faith in May 1943 — Radnóti was deemed a Jew and subject to far-reaching restrictions.

The 'Law on Assuring a More Balanced Social and Economic Life' — the 'First Jewish Law' — was passed by Hungary's Parliament on 29 May 1938. The statute introduced strict limits on the proportion of Jews who could be employed as publishers, editors, or journalists, as well as on the proportion of Jews permitted to work in the theatre and film industries.[6] Although Radnóti could continue to publish reviews, essays, and poems on a freelance basis, he was effectively precluded from joining the permanent staff of a journal or newspaper, which would have provided him with a regular salary. Because of Radnóti's Jewish origins, a teaching post was also out of the question, despite his impressive academic qualifications. Radnóti's modest income consisted of limited financial support from relatives, as well as monies earned from private tutoring and occasional freelance work for publishers. From 1939, with the enactment of the so-called 'Second Jewish Law', or 'Law for the Limitation of the Jewish Occupation of Public and Economic Affairs', Radnóti's ability to support himself from journalism or teaching was further curtailed.[7]

Despite the psychological and economic impact of Hungary's Jewish Laws, which treated Jews as alien and unwelcome, Radnóti stubbornly persisted in seeing himself as 'just a Hungarian poet'. In one of his most celebrated later poems, *Nem tudhatom* (*I Cannot Know*), completed in January 1944, he gave voice to an exasperated but abiding love for his homeland, a country that had rejected him, consigning Radnóti to pariah status. Here are the opening lines of the poem in my own translation:

I have no way of knowing what this land may mean to others,
But for me this small country, bathed in fire, is my birthplace,
It's the far-off world of my childhood.
I emerged from this land like a delicate shoot from a tree,
And I hope that, in time, my body will sink back into this earth.
I am at home here.

In an earlier poem, *Nyugtalan orán* (*In a Restless Hour*), completed in January 1939, just months after the passage of the First Jewish Law, he ponders whether, like the 'mute stones' amongst which he now finds himself, he should embrace silence? 'Tell me,' he cries, 'what would induce me to write poetry now? Death?'

Fortunately for future generations, Radnóti could not remain silent in the face of the savagery and injustices that he witnessed and even experienced at first hand. Rather than opting to remain mute, he became the doomed yet inspired chronicler of the collapse of humane, civilized values in his homeland and across much of Europe. As Radnóti declared in a poem entitled *Töredék* (*Fragment*), which he completed in May 1944, just months before he was murdered by his Hungarian guards: 'I lived on this earth at a time/ when informing was considered a virtue and the murderer/ the traitor and the robber were heroes'.

*Simon Leichner at the Jewish Community
Centre in Sighet, March 2006*

'I was conscripted into a labour battalion,' Simon Leichner tells me in fluent Hungarian when I visit him at his village home in Ocna Şugatag, Romania.[8] Simon, whom I had been introduced to at the Jewish Community Centre in nearby Sighet, was born in 1922. He was just eighteen years old when Hungarian troops reoccupied northern Transylvania, including Ocna Şugatag and Sighet, in 1940. Following mediation by Germany and Italy, Romania ceded a large tranche of territory to Hungary, amounting to 43,000 square kilometres. The Second Vienna Award, as the settlement came to be known, enabled Hungary to recover a significant portion of the land that had been lost to Romania in the peace settlement following World War One.[9]

Later, in Sighet, I am introduced to Magda, an ethnic Hungarian who has spent her whole life in the little town that adjoins Romania's border with the Ukraine. 'Things really started to change when the Hungarian troops arrived here!' Magda tells me.[10]

A spry woman in her eighties, just two years younger than Simon, Magda chain smokes as she prepares lunch for me and for Öcsi, her middle-aged son, in their rambling old home. Recently widowed and in his late fifties, Öcsi tells me that he bought the property, located in the centre of Sighet, from two elderly Jewish spinsters. The women, who had survived deportation to Auschwitz, had no living relatives. Weary of living in such a draughty old house, they'd decided to sell the property and move into a modern apartment in a Ceauşescu-era *bloc*.

'The Hungarian soldiers immediately set to work to improve the town's flood defences,' Magda tells me, as she stirs soup in a large enamel pot. 'The Romanians didn't do anything in all the years they were here!'

Known as Sziget — 'island' — in Hungarian, the town derives its name from the fact that it's almost entirely enclosed by two rivers, the Tisza and the Iza. For as long as anyone could remember, Sighet had been subject to severe flooding.

Magda, like most of her family and friends, was thrilled by the restoration of Hungarian rule over Northern Transylvania. But there was unease amongst the territory's 138,000 Jews, who were keenly aware of the growing climate of anti-Semitism in Hungary and of the raft of anti-Jewish legislation that had been enacted in recent years. In addition to the First and Second Jewish Laws, these included measures conscripting able-bodied Jewish men into specially constituted auxiliary labour battalions.[11] As labour servicemen, Jews were routinely required to dig anti-tank ditches, carry munitions, help to build roads and bridges, load and unload freight trains, and work in mines.

According to the American historian Raul Hilberg, as many as 130,000 Jewish men may have served in Hungary's auxiliary labour battalions during World War Two.[12] Of these, up to 40,000 died, many of exhaustion, disease, malnutrition, or starvation. Withholding part — even a substantial part — of men's rations was not uncommon. For example, Ferenc Pándi, a labour serviceman stationed in the village of Sianki in Sub-Carpathian Ruthenia, wrote in his diary: 'Our food [ration] for a day looks quite good on paper... but the reality is different. For example, yesterday's supper was plain bean soup with six to seven beans. It was almost like plain water.'[13] Others died as a result of brutal and sadistic treatment by their Hungarian officers and NCOs. In his detailed account of Hungary's auxiliary labour system, Randolph Braham recounts numerous examples of ill-treatment, including the fate of a unit of labour servicemen stationed in occupied Soviet territory:[14]

Some of the guards amused themselves by hosing down the Jews in winter until they became 'ice statues' or by tying them onto tree branches with their hands tied against their backs. These, and many other similarly cruel 'amusements', were normally carried out after the Jews had returned from their work.

German army officers who witnessed the treatment of labour servicemen by Hungarian officers and NCOs were appalled. They repeatedly warned their Hungarian counterparts that they had to choose between beating the Jews or using them as an effective workforce.[15]

Unlike many of his peers, Simon Leichner was lucky. When I ask him whether his unit, comprising between two hundred and fifty and three hundred Jews, had been given insufficient or inedible food, Simon shakes his head emphatically. 'No, we always had good food, decent food,' he says. 'We didn't go hungry or anything like that. Definitely not! We were fed three times a day — in the morning, at lunchtime, and in the evening. And there was always a decent amount of bread.'

Even so, life as an auxiliary labour serviceman was far from easy for some of the Jews in Simon's company, particularly those who were unaccustomed to manual labour. 'There were doctors and other well-off people from Budapest,' he tells me. 'They weren't used to the kind of rough work we had to do… They were *uriemberek*, gentlefolk.'

Six days a week Simon and his company felled logs in the forests, built bunkers, and dug holes for landmines in a desperate bid to impede the Soviet Red Army's advance. However, on Sundays, some of the men from Simon's company would put on a show. 'The Hungarian soldiers really appreciated it,' Simon tells me, smiling. 'They were good shows!'

'Was there music?'

'Some people played instruments, some sang, others danced.'

'Were people forced to perform?' I ask. I had a mental image of the Jewish musicians in Nazi concentration camps who were ordered to play for their guards and fellow inmates.[16]

'Not a bit of it!' says Simon. 'Our life wasn't bad at all. It was bad for those who were taken away [to the death camps].'

'What about the Hungarian NCOs and officers who commanded your company?' I ask. 'Were they violent or abusive?'

'No, not really. They were fine.'

And clothes, did they issue you with clothes and proper boots?' Although the situation was to improve later that year while Vilmos Nagy was briefly Hungary's Minister of Defence, 'practically all of the labour servicemen served in their own civilian clothes and footwear' by the early months of 1942.[17] Inevitably, these became tattered and worn as a result of prolonged and intensive use, particularly in the arduous conditions encountered in the Ukraine. At the same time, many labour conscripts, desperately hungry on account of their meagre and irregular rations, which were not always provided in full, bartered some of their clothing for food.

'They gave us clothes,' says Simon, although he remembers that the garments were thin and of poor quality. 'Perhaps some of the clothes came from Auschwitz?' he muses. After the War, he met several camp survivors who had returned to their homes in Sighet and the surrounding villages. Simon learned from these men, as well as from photographs in newspapers, that the inmates at Auschwitz had been issued with threadbare striped uniforms. 'That's the type of clothes we were given,' he says.

— ⁓ —

Miklós Radnóti was conscripted into a Hungarian auxiliary labour battalion in September 1940 when he was thirty-one years of age. Unlike Simon Leichner, who was accustomed to manual labour and to being outdoors in all weathers, Radnóti's working life had been spent as an editor, poet, and literary translator. A medical examination, conducted just weeks after Radnóti was called up, revealed that he was suffering from two hernias. Even so, army doctors ruled that he was well enough to remain with his unit, despite the strenuous nature of the work that the labour conscripts routinely performed.[18]

Until mid-December 1940, when Radnóti was discharged, he was deployed with his comrades in various locations, including territory newly recovered from Romania. His unit's duties involved dismantling the defensive positions that had been constructed by Romanian troops, including wire fences and metal posts. Whether through bureaucratic indifference or a genuine lack of resources, Radnóti and his fellow labour servicemen were not provided with tools or even gloves and were reduced to working with their bare hands.[19]

In summer 1942 Radnóti was called up again, serving until May of the following year. Initially, he was despatched to a region vacated by Romania. Subsequently, Radnóti was sent to an arms factory in northern Hungary and then to a machine workshop in Újpest, close to the capital. While posted in Újpest, he was routinely granted permission to sleep at home in the small apartment he shared with Fanni, his wife. However, in contrast to his earlier period of labour service, Radnóti was now required to wear a yellow armband at all times that immediately identified him as a Jew.[20]

In March 1943, while Radnóti was waiting at a tram stop in Budapest, a reserve army officer noticed the yellow armband and ordered the poet to accompany him to the nearby Albrecht barracks. Over the course of several hours a group of jeering Hungarian soldiers beat and humiliated Radnóti, together with two other Jewish labour conscripts. Before Radnóti was released his hair was roughly shorn off, giving him the appearance of a convict. As an additional indignity, he was forced to pay the barber for his 'services'. Radnóti was severely traumatised by the incident. He ceased making entries in his diary and only resumed writing poetry after an interval of several months.

Radnóti was called up a third and final time in May 1944, serving until his death in November. During this period, he worked in various locations, including the infamous copper mine at Bor in present-day Serbia. The mine, which contained huge reserves of copper and other precious metals, was of considerable importance to the German war effort, particularly after Axis troops were forced to withdraw completely from Soviet territory.

Radnóti composed his *Seventh Eclogue*, one of his most beautiful and moving poems, while stationed at Lager Heidenau, close to Bor. As the exhausted men around him slept, he remained awake, crafting verses of extraordinary poignancy and power. The *Seventh Eclogue* takes us right into the night-time barracks with its snoring, ragged labour servicemen lying asleep on narrow wooden boards. The men long for their distant homes while uneasily aware that they may have been destroyed along with the familiar, civilized world to which they belonged — casualties of a brutal and remorseless war: 'Tell me, does that home still exist where they know what a hexameter is?' The *Seventh Eclogue* also allows us to glimpse the petty privations to which the labour conscripts were subjected by their guards:[21]

> Without commas, one line touching the other,
> I write poems the way I live, in darkness,
> blind, crossing the paper like a worm.
> Flashlights, books — the guards took everything.
> There's no mail, only fog drifts over the barracks.

The Hungarian labour conscripts at Bor toiled alongside 'Serbian convicts, Greek and Russian prisoners' as well as Italians.[22] There were also ultra-Orthodox Jews from Sub-Carpathian Ruthenia and present-day Slovakia, as well as Christians, mostly Seventh-Day Adventists and Jehovah's Witnesses, who had refused to bear arms.

Conditions at Bor were unremittingly harsh. In his history of the Hungarian Holocaust, Randolph Braham records that the labour servicemen 'worked under gruelling conditions for about 11 hours a day, receiving 7 *dinars* and half a pound of bread and a portion of watery soup per day in compensation'.[23] Braham notes that a number of the Hungarian officers and NCOs accompanying the men 'distinguished themselves by their cruelty', while some even stole their rations.[24]

One of Radnóti's final poems, *Forced March*, was written in September 1944, just days before the poet and many of his comrades were evacuated on foot from Bor as the Soviet Red Army drew closer. 'Only a fool collapses in a heap on the ground, gets up and trudges on,' begins the poem. Instead of remaining where he is, the labour conscript in Radnóti's poem hurries to rejoin the column of exhausted men. 'Why?' someone asks him. 'Because my wife is waiting for me,' comes the answer, 'and a better, more beautiful death'.

A contingent of 2,600 labour servicemen, escorted by Hungarian soldiers, left Bor on foot on 29 September.

Ambushed by Yugoslav partisans, the Hungarian guards surrendered. The partisans freed the labour conscripts, who were provided with food and shelter by local civilians until arrangements could be made to transport them to Timişoara in western Romania, pending their eventual repatriation to Hungary.[25]

Radnóti had left Bor almost two weeks earlier with a large group of labour servicemen and an armed escort. The column, which was 'driven mercilessly with little or no food and water', headed towards Belgrade.[26] Serbian civilians, moved by the men's plight, tried to offer help. After a lengthy halt in Belgrade, the column made its way, in stages, towards Crvenka in northern Serbia. Pausing for three days in the town of Novi Sad, Radnóti and his fellow labour conscripts were given no food by their guards. In their desperation, some of them resorted to eating straw that they managed to boil on an old stove.[27]

In Crvenka, an SS unit methodically murdered several hundred men from the column who were viewed as surplus to requirements.[28] The rest, including Radnóti, 'whose feet were covered with open wounds' and who was racked by horrific toothache, were marched to the southern Hungarian town of Mohács. From Mohács, a train took Radnóti and the other survivors to Szentkirályszabadja.

Those who saw and spoke to Radnóti at this time, including a fellow labour serviceman who had known the poet in Szeged, later remarked that he appeared weak and listless and that his shoes were completely worn out.[29] On the road leading to Mohács, Radnóti is thought to have parted with his wedding ring, giving it to a labour conscript who had promised him food. In the event, Radnóti received nothing.

The precise details of Radnóti's onward journey from Szentkirályszabadja towards the Austrian border remain unknown. He and his comrades almost certainly set out on foot in the first week of November, although Radnóti, along with others too ill or exhausted to walk, may have been transferred to horse-drawn carts requisitioned for the purpose.

According to several accounts, Radnóti was taken to the town of Győr together with a number of other men in urgent need of medical attention.[30] But the hospitals in Győr, already overwhelmed with the sick and injured, refused to admit them. At this point, Cadet Sergeant András Tálas, commander of the Hungarian soldiers escorting Radnóti and his ailing comrades, took the decision to dispose of them on the grounds that they could be of no further use.[31] On or about 9 November 1944, at the village of Abda, twenty-two labour conscripts, including Radnóti, were summarily executed, each with a bullet to the nape of the neck. The bodies were hastily buried in an unmarked grave.

In June 1946, when the communal grave was exhumed, one of the corpses was described as male, with light brown hair and several missing upper front teeth, as well as a crowned lower tooth. The body was officially identified as: 'Radnóczi (Radnóti) Miklós poet Budapest, Pozsonyi út 1-4'.[32] Among the personal possessions found with Radnóti was a small, yellowed notebook containing his final, agonized verses, including a cycle of four terse poems entitled *Razglednicák*, a Serbian word meaning 'postcard'. *Razglednicák* is both an ironic allusion to the brevity of the poems and to the fact that they were written while Radnóti was far from home and from Fanni, his wife. Consisting of just a few lines each, stripped to their bare poetic essence, Radnóti's 'postcards' convey the futility and brutishness of war as well as the awful fate of Hungary's auxiliary labour servicemen.

The very last poem Radnóti composed was written on a scrap of paper inserted in the notebook. It is dated 31 October 1944, and Radnóti has written 'Szentkirályszabadja' next to the date. In the poem, which is all the more powerful because of its starkly unsentimental tone, he depicts the random murder of a comrade and foresees his own imminent death:

I threw myself down beside him and his body rolled over
already taut like a string about to snap.
Shot in the nape of the neck. 'That's how you'll end up too!'
I whispered to myself. 'Just lie here quietly,
patience will blossom into death'.
'*Der springt noch auf*', someone called out above.
My ear was caked with mud and drying blood.

—※—

My mother (middle row, far left) with Zoli Füredi (front left)
and friends in the Buda hills, 1943

'I was coming home from work,' says my mother. 'At the time, we were still living in Uncle Ármin's apartment. We had nowhere else to go.'

In Hungary, the War had been over for several months but neither Ármin nor his wife and children had returned to reclaim their two-room apartment on Kresz Géza *utca*, leaving my mother, uncle, and grandmother in sole possession. According to Ármin's younger brother Bertalan, Ármin had died of a heart attack on the outskirts of Budapest while serving in an auxiliary labour battalion during the latter stages of the War. His wife and teenage children had almost certainly perished during the late autumn or winter of 1944, whether at the hands of Arrow Cross thugs or in the cramped and disease-ridden Jewish ghetto established in Budapest in December 1944.

'I was just about to enter the building when a young woman, one of our neighbours, happened to come out,' continues my mother. '"Hurry home!" she exclaimed when she caught sight of me. "You're going to have a wonderful surprise!"'

My mother, thinking that her father had returned, raced up the stone steps to her apartment. As recounted previously, teenage Arrow Cross militiamen had hustled Miklós away at gunpoint in early November 1944, along with several other Jewish men who were still living in the building. My mother and her family continued to hope that, despite the passage of so much time, Miklós might still be alive, perhaps interned in a displaced persons' camp in Germany or Austria. After the War, thousands of Jewish slave labourers, including many from Hungary, had ended up in these camps.

'But it wasn't Miklós,' says my mother, with a sigh. 'When I opened the front door to our flat I came face to face with Zoli Füredi!'

My mother's disappointment at not being reunited with her father was mixed with joy at seeing Zoli, to whom she'd become engaged while in her final year at the Kőszegi Dobó Womens' Commercial School in Budapest. Following a brief and intense courtship, which culminated in the young couple resolving to marry as soon as my mother obtained her school leaving certificate, Zoli had been conscripted into an auxiliary labour battalion. He had been sent far away with his unit, and he and my mother had lost touch. In the months since the end of the War there had been no word from Zoli, leading my mother to conclude that he'd either died or that he'd chosen to return to Nové Zámky, the small town in Czechoslovakia where his parents owned a shop and where Zoli had spent his childhood.

'We kissed and clung to one another for ages!' recalls my mother. 'Afterwards, we sat down and Zoli told me what had happened to him.'

Like Miklós Radnóti, Zoli and his unit of labour servicemen had been taken to Bor. Physically strong and tough-minded, Zoli had been set to work in the mine. Despite appalling conditions and confrontations with his guards Zoli had survived, while many around him had succumbed to disease, malnutrition, and exhaustion.

'Zoli took out a crumpled black and white photograph from an inside pocket of his jacket,' continues my mother. 'It was a photo of me. I'd given it to Zoli shortly before he and his unit left Budapest.'

Zoli told my mother that he'd kept the photo with him at Bor and throughout the entire time that he'd been a labour serviceman. 'The guards tried to take it from him, but he refused to let them have it,' says my mother. 'Zoli said that they gave him a terrible beating because he wouldn't hand over my photograph.'

Whether this anecdote is entirely true or whether Zoli embellished it to impress my mother, I can't say. But it undoubtedly had its intended effect, rekindling my mother's ardour.

After he was liberated, Zoli's first impulse had been to go to Nové Zámky to look for his parents. An only child, he clung to the hope that his parents were still alive and that he'd find them living in the little town. But Zoli had been forced to wait until Soviet forces had expelled German troops and their Hungarian allies from Slovak territory.

'Zoli went to Érsekújvár as soon as he could travel there,' says my mother, using the Hungarian name for Nové Zámky. 'But he couldn't find any trace of his parents and he had no idea where else to look for them.'

Although Zoli was unwilling to accept the fact, his parents had almost certainly perished along with most of the Jews of Nové Zámky. In March 1944, German troops had occupied Hungary, a nominal ally, as a result of mounting concern that Hungary's leaders were secretly negotiating a separate armistice with the Allies. In April, after discussions involving high-ranking Hungarian and German officials, the Hungarian government issued a decree authorising the confinement of the country's Jewish population in ghettos.[33] The decree applied to Nové Zámky and to much of what is now the southern part of Slovakia, which had been 'reunited' with Hungary in 1938.

In late May, Zoli's parents, together with other Jews living in Nové Zámky, were taken to a newly established ghetto in the centre of the town.[34] In the first week of June, the occupants were transferred to a second and larger ghetto that had been constructed at the town's former Grünfeld brickworks, joining Jews from the surrounding villages. After enduring appalling conditions in the Grünfeld camp, including the lack of sufficient drinking water, 4,843 Jews were herded into goods wagons and sent from Nové Zámky to Auschwitz-Birkenau in mid-June. Of these, 4,386 died, whether as a result of gassing, malnutrition, disease, or other causes.[35] Zoli's parents were almost certainly amongst the dead.

'After spending some time in Nové Zámky looking for his parents, Zoli decided to come to Budapest to search for me,' continues my mother. 'At that point, he didn't even know if I was alive'.

Reunited once more, the young couple soon began to plan a future together. 'We were going to get married and move to Nové Zámky,' says my mother. 'Zoli told me he wanted to reopen his parents' shop.'

'What happened?' I ask. 'Why didn't the marriage go ahead?'

My mother pauses. 'For a few months, Zoli commuted between Budapest and Nové Zámky,' she tells me. 'He still believed that his parents might be alive and that they would eventually return to their home.' On these visits to Nové Zámky, Zoli lodged with a Jewish widow whose husband and child had perished in the Holocaust. Although older than Zoli by several years, the widow was said to be attractive.

'We didn't argue or anything, but all of a sudden Zoli stopped coming to see me,' says my mother. 'I tried looking for him, but he was nowhere to be found. In the end, I convinced myself that Zoli had been arrested, that his frequent trips across the border had aroused the suspicions of the Czechoslovak border guards. Perhaps they suspected him of involvement in smuggling or in some other illegal activity.'

'And how did you learn the truth?'

'Etelka could see the state I was in. I'd been on the verge of getting married when suddenly my fiancé disappears without warning,' continues my mother. 'Etelka pleaded with someone she knew, the husband of a relative, to go to Nové Zámky to make inquiries. Feri had grown up in Bratislava. He spoke Slovak and Hungarian fluently.'

'Was he able to discover anything?'

'Yes. Feri was told that Zoli and the widow had left Nové Zámky together. With the help of the *Bricha*, an underground Jewish organisation, they'd set out for Palestine.'

In the aftermath of the War, such clandestine voyages to Palestine were long, acutely uncomfortable, and hazardous. Because of the continuing opposition of Great Britain, which governed Palestine until mid-May 1948, Jewish immigrants were often crammed into old and unsuitable vessels for the illicit sea crossing. There was a very real risk of drowning or of being intercepted by British warships and of being hauled off to a detention camp in Cyprus or Germany. But Zoli and the widow, in common with tens of thousands of Jews who'd lost loved ones in the Holocaust, were overcome by an urge to leave Europe and to rebuild their lives elsewhere. My mother, for whom the ideological abstractions of Zionism held no appeal, remained in the city of her birth. She never heard from Zoli again.

16

Why my great-uncle Ágoston
owed his life to football

Didn't your father consider fleeing abroad before it was too late?' I ask Ági. My first cousin once removed has just told me that, by the mid 1930s, her father, Ágoston Weisz, had saved up a little money and had formed numerous foreign connections through his work with one of Budapest's leading football clubs, MTK. According to Ági, her father was a popular and respected figure in football circles, passionately devoted to his club.

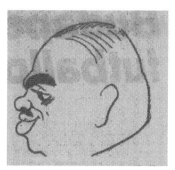

Drawing of Ágoston Weisz in
Nemzeti Sport, 23 February, 1937

'My father could have gone anywhere if he'd wanted to!' Ági tells me. 'Anywhere! Until the very end of his life, people he'd coached or helped in some way would write to him from around the world. If they were visiting Hungary, they'd always come to see him.'

I couldn't help wondering whether Ági may have had an exaggerated sense of her father's prominence in Hungarian football in the years leading up to World War Two. I could find no mention of Ágoston Weisz on MTK's website, where the achievements of several footballers and coaches from the inter-war era are recorded. Like Ágoston, many of them had been of Jewish descent. Béla Gárdos (né Guttmann) had played for MTK in the early 1920s before going on to become a highly respected and innovative coach. Aside from his native Hungary, Gárdos had worked with well-known clubs in Austria, Holland, Italy, Portugal, and Greece, as well as in such football-crazed countries as Uruguay, Argentina, and Brazil.

While Gárdos, who barely escaped transportation to Auschwitz-Birkenau, lived to an advanced age, other Hungarian-Jewish footballers were less fortunate. Antal Vágó (né Weisz) represented his country at the 1912 Olympic Games in Stockholm, where the Hungarian football team was placed fifth overall. Vágó's playing career with MTK — he appeared no less than 180 times for the club — stretched

A Match at MTK's stadium, 1929

from 1911 until 1923. Along with thousands of Budapest's Jews, he was murdered by *Nyilas* militiamen on the banks of the Danube in December 1944.[36]

The fate of Árpád Weisz was even worse. After playing for teams in Hungary and Italy, including Alessandria FC and Milano, Weisz became the inspirational coach of Bologna FC, which he led to unprecedented success in the 1930s. Forced to leave Italy following the passage of stringent anti-Jewish laws, Weisz joined Dordrecht, in the Netherlands, as the club's trainer. The German occupation of the Netherlands in 1940 led to strict curbs on the employment of Jews, obliging Weisz to relinquish his post. Unable to find alternative work, he struggled to support his family. In due course, together with his wife and children Árpád Weisz was interned in a camp for Dutch Jews established at Westerbork. From there, the family was transported to Auschwitz-Birkenau, where they were murdered.[37]

My great uncle Ágoston was neither a football player of exceptional talent nor an internationally sought-after coach. Even so, I came to realise that my cousin had not overstated her father's achievements. After combing through newspaper archives and corresponding with MTK, I learnt that Ágoston Weisz, or 'Ági' as he was universally known in football circles, had been a familiar, respected, and generally well-liked figure. There are literally hundreds of references to Ági in Hungarian sports papers, including *Nemzeti Sport* and *Sporthírlap*, throughout the 1920s and 1930s. Ágoston had worked tirelessly as a club official and as an increasingly influential voice in the Hungarian Football Federation, while coaching top amateur teams in his spare time. In February 1937, an article in *Nemzeti Sport*, quoting his remarks about a forthcoming match, was accompanied by a pen and ink drawing of Ágoston. Although hardly flattering, the caricature was clearly intended to be affectionate.

Ágoston's diligence, organisational talents, and leadership qualities had been recognised before World War One by Fradi, the first club with which he was associated. At just eighteen years of age, Ágoston was appointed manager of Fradi's youth team, an unusually onerous position for someone so young. Yet the turmoil and political upheavals that shook Hungary in the aftermath of World War One caused an irreparable breach between Ágoston and the club. A brief article in *Sporthírlap* noted that several key figures, including Ágoston, left Fradi in September 1919 because of what the newspaper coyly described as 'the manifestation of confessional tendencies' at the club.[38] In reality, a series of anti-Semitic incidents had prompted Ágoston and a number of other Jews to quit.

The incidents at Fradi were part of a tsunami of anti-Semitism that engulfed Hungary following the collapse of a short-lived Communist government that August. The Communists' radical and frequently unpopular policies, as recounted earlier, had been accompanied by numerous acts of violence and intimidation. Well over a dozen Hungarian Jews, including Béla Kun, had played a prominent role in the Communist regime — a fact that was eagerly seized upon by the reactionary forces that gained control of Hungary in late summer 1919. Although Ágoston had remained aloof from the Communist administration headed by Kun, he and other Jews at Fradi were treated with open hostility by some of their club colleagues.

Ágoston's decision to leave Fradi was made easier by an offer from Alfréd Brüll, a wealthy Jewish industrialist and President of Fradi's arch-rival, MTK. Initially appointed manager of MTK's youth team, Ágoston subsequently oversaw the running of the club's stadium, also finding time to coach top-level amateur teams. Fluent in German thanks to his mother Jerta, a native German speaker, Ágoston was regularly called upon to welcome foreign football teams arriving in Budapest. However, his most significant contribution to the sport was his work with the Hungarian Football Federation. For many years, Ágoston served as head of the HFF's disciplinary committee, enjoying a reputation for sternness allied with fair-mindedness.[39]

'So what held your father back?' I ask Ági. 'With all the foreign connections he'd made through football why didn't he leave Hungary while it was still possible?'

'My father once told me that he was born here and that he'd always considered himself Hungarian,' Ági says. 'He simply couldn't imagine living anywhere else'. Stubborn, patriotic, and intensely proud, Ágoston viewed flight abroad as cowardly and unwarranted.

Ági begins to rifle through a pile of documents on the table in front of her, extracting one with a flourish. 'Look!' she says. 'My father was called up on 24 November 1940. He was assigned to military headquarters in Munkács.'

Now the bustling, medium-sized city of Munkachevo in southwest Ukraine, Munkács belonged to Hungary until World War One. Awarded to Czechoslovakia in the post-war peace settlement, together with a large strip of Hungarian territory, it was restored to Hungary in November 1938 along with much of southern Slovakia. Budapest sent troops to the area, known in Hungary as the *Felvidék*, to assure Hungarian sovereignty and to facilitate a smooth transition.

Ágoston's military service in Munkács barely lasted a few weeks. On 5 January 1941, he was abruptly relieved of his duties and sent home. Late the following month, he was notified by letter that he had been discharged from

Hungary's reserve forces, in which he held the rank of *Tartalékos Zászlós* or Reserve Officer Cadet.

'Why was your father discharged?'

Ági searches for another letter. 'Yes, here it is!' she exclaims. The word *ZSIDÓ* — JEW — is written in large red letters in the space after 'Reason for Discharge'. Later that year, all Jewish career officers serving in the Hungarian army were formally stripped of their rank.

No longer protected by his status as a reserve army officer and despite his age and physical infirmity, Ágoston was conscripted into an auxiliary labour battalion. However, Ági can't tell me anything about her father's experiences other than the fact that he served with a unit in Szigetmon-ostor, a village in Pest county. 'Dad didn't really talk about these things,' Ági says, 'unless I made a point of sitting down beside him and asking him questions. I suppose he just wanted to forget.'

In late autumn 1944, after a German-engineered coup that brought Ferenc Szálasi and the *Nyilaskeresztes* or Arrow Cross Party to power, Budapest's Jews, having narrowly escaped transportation to Auschwitz-Birkenau in the early summer, once again faced an existential threat. *Nyilas* militiamen plundered and murdered Jews at will, while the Szálasi regime initiated a series of ominous measures. As described in greater detail elsewhere, tens of thousands of Budapest's Jews, earmarked for slave labour in the Reich, were sent on death marches to Germany, a journey of seven or eight days. Despite severe cold and frequent rain, the Jews, including women as well as men, were rarely provided with food or shelter.[40] Those who couldn't keep up were shot by their Hungarian guards.

Ágoston, who had returned to Budapest after he was discharged from labour service, was picked up by an Arrow Cross patrol, along with other Jewish men in his apartment building. Taken to the Óbuda brickworks, where Jews were held for two or three days before setting out on the death march to Germany, he faced appalling conditions:[41]

> Thousands were kept in the brick-drying barns (which had roofs but no walls) and many others were compelled to stay in the rain in the courtyard. They were not given any food and the *Nyilas*, who exercised real power although nominally the police were entrusted with keeping order, robbed them of their valuables, clothing, blankets, and whatever supplies they had.

It's far from certain that Ágoston, who was almost fifty years old and whose mobility was seriously impaired by his war injury, would have survived the week-long trek to the German border, particularly after spending some days at the Óbuda brickworks without food and exposed to the elements. Dejected and bewildered, he was unexpectedly saved by a *Nyilas* guard. A keen amateur footballer, the guard recognised Ágoston amongst the new arrivals at the brickyard.

'Uncle Ági!' the guard exclaimed. 'What are you doing here? Come with me and I'll let you out!'

For that *Nyilas* guard, the fraternal bonds inspired by familiarity and by a mutual love of football were stronger and more enduring than the hate-filled dogmas of the Arrow Cross. In his eyes, Uncle Ági remained, first and foremost, an exemplary coach and a fellow football enthusiast, rather than a Jew. 'You were always good to me,' the guard said, as he led Ágoston out of the brickyard.

Despite evading the forced march to Germany, Ágoston remained in grave danger. By early December, along with the overwhelming majority of Budapest's Jews, Ágoston had been compelled to move into a hastily constructed ghetto that the Arrow Cross authorities established in the

Seventh District.† Surrounded by a high wooden fence, the entire ghetto comprised just 0.3 square kilometres. By the end of December, it contained 55,000 Jews, a figure that rose to almost 70,000 in the following month.[42]

With limited and increasingly irregular supplies of food, water, and fuel, chronic overcrowding, inadequate sanitation, the constant accumulation of rubbish, and repeated incursions by armed elements, conditions in the ghetto were precarious, at best. However, they deteriorated sharply after Soviet forces succeeded in encircling Budapest in December, initiating a siege that was to last for several weeks.

Jews in the ghetto now had to contend with acute and worsening shortages of drinking water, food, and fuel. Dr. Sándor Bródy, who was transferred to the main ghetto from the international ghetto in the first week of January along with thousands of other Jews, described the conditions he encountered:[43]

Eleven of us found shelter in one of the storerooms on Wesselényi Street that belonged to the Universal Furniture Store. Here, in complete darkness, we shivered, hungered and thirsted for the next two weeks. The electricity didn't work. Neither did the water system. In the entire ghetto there were just a few cellars where a little water dribbled from the taps. We were only allowed outside for two hours a day but, during that period, thousands

† A second and smaller ghetto, comprising various apartment buildings near St. István Park, was established for 'protected' Jews who held papers issued by the Vatican or by one of the handful of neutral foreign legations in Budapest. In reality, approximately 15,000 'protected' Jews enjoyed little or no protection, while their living conditions were horrendous. Two-room apartments routinely accommodated between fifty and sixty people.

would crowd around the taps with basins, heedless of the constant shelling and the machinegun bullets sprayed by the aircraft flying overhead.

The ghetto's beleaguered Jews also faced a growing threat from marauding armed bands, who murdered and robbed at will.[44] On 5 January 1945, two armed men dressed in civilian clothes entered the ghetto, shooting and killing a Jewish woman on Rumbach Sebestyén *utca*. On the following day a large group of armed men, some of whom were wearing Arrow Cross armbands, robbed the occupants of an apartment building at 4 Wesselényi *utca*, murdering the Jewish head of the building when he tried to intervene. The next day, two armed men, apparently wearing armbands, made their way into the ghetto, killing an elderly Jewish woman they encountered on the street. A few days afterwards, 43 Jews were massacred at 27 Wesselényi *utca* by *Nyilas* militiamen.

With his ample frame and imposing height, Ágoston might easily have perished in the ghetto from lack of food if it had not been for Ági's mother, Juliska. A simple peasant woman, Juliska had been hired by Ágoston as a live-in maid some years before the War. Juliska's duties had included helping to look after Ágoston's sickly wife, Rezsina. A divorced woman, two years older than Ágoston, she died in the late 1930s due to complications from a lung infection. Juliska had stayed on in the spacious, three-room apartment on Visegrád *utca* as Ágoston's housekeeper. At some point, Juliska and Ágoston became lovers.

In late March 1944, a decree issued by Hungary's quisling government prohibiting non-Jews from working in Jewish households compelled Juliska to find alternative accommodation and a new job.[45] However, Juliska and Ágoston remained in close touch. After Ágoston was interned in the

Jewish ghetto, Juliska took him parcels of food and clean clothes as often as she could.

'Was that allowed?' I ask Ági.

'Yes, at least for a while,' she says. 'Only small parcels, though. And there were strict rules about how often you were allowed to bring provisions and which gate you had to take them to.'

As the siege of Budapest intensified, with heavy and prolonged artillery barrages that left much of the city in ruins, almost all contact between the ghetto's terrified occupants and the outside world ceased. Supplies of food and other essentials dwindled, leading to a sharp increase in the daily tally of deaths from starvation.[46]

'My father was tall and thickset. He was a big, heavy man,' says Ági. 'But when he emerged from the ghetto, after it was liberated by the Russians, he couldn't have weighed more than 50 kilos, much less than half of what he'd been before'. Barely two months later, on 17 March 1945, Ágoston and Juliska were married. Ági, their only child, was born several years afterwards.

—⁂—

'My paternal grandfather was a *kocsmáros*, an innkeeper, in Petőpuszta,' Edit tells me. 'He fell off a horse-drawn cart while it was travelling at speed and died on the spot'.

'Was he drunk?'

Edit seems surprised and even a little offended by my question. 'No, it was an accident,' she says firmly, although I wonder how she can be so certain.

At the time of her grandfather's unexpected death, Petőpuszta, a rural settlement in what is now the Slovak municipality of Kováčovce, was part of Austria-Hungary. Many of the local people, particularly peasants and agricultural labourers, were ethnic Slovaks. By contrast, public officials and most of the owners of landed estates in the surrounding region were Hungarian. Many of the shopkeepers and innkeepers were Jews. The area was a microcosm of the Dual Empire in which a jumble of peoples, speaking a multitude of languages and worshipping in an assortment of churches, synagogues, and prayer halls, coexisted with varying degrees of amicability and mutual tolerance.

'After my grandfather's death my grandmother decided to leave Petőpuszta for good,' Edit continues. 'Together with her children, two girls and two boys, she boarded a train bound for Budapest.'

Even though he had only been an infant at the time, Edit's father would always remember that train journey and its dreadful aftermath. Arriving at the bustling Nyugati railway station in Budapest, their throats parched, the family had paused at a drinking fountain to wash the grime from their faces and to slake their thirst. Barefooted, his prized boots slung around his neck, Edit's father had placed his footwear by the edge of the fountain before leaning forward to drink. Moments later, reaching for his boots, he burst into tears on realising that they'd been stolen by an opportunistic thief.

'My grandmother found work in a bakery and my aunts were apprenticed to a hatter,' Edit tells me. 'But the family was too poor to support my father while he continued his studies.' Aged ten, having completed just two years of schooling, Edit's father took a job in a factory making enamel pots and pans.

'He was incredibly handsome, charming and quick-witted!' says Edit, recalling her father, whom she plainly adored. 'He was so good-looking and he always dressed so elegantly, with his hand-stitched shoes. Women would follow him in the street, even beautiful women, actresses. They couldn't help themselves!'

Having started out as a juvenile factory worker, without skills or qualifications of any kind, Edit's father went on to become a salesman with the prestigious Manfred Weiss Steel and Metal Works, one of the largest and most important industrial enterprises in Hungary. Eager to strike out on his own, he acquired a shop selling electrical goods. Some years later, he became the owner of a small factory producing high-quality white cement.

Edit is recounting her family history over lunch at one of the smart bistros that have sprung up on Pozsonyi út in the Újlipótváros district of Budapest. Just a few yards from Edit's apartment, Pozsonyi út has played a prominent role in Edit's long and eventful life.

'I was nearly eight years old and living with my parents in Budapest when the *Nyilas* seized power,' says Edit, who was born in December 1936. Led by Ferenc Szálasi, an ex-officer in the Hungarian army, the Arrow Cross Party was a Nazi-style political movement, fervently anti-Communist as well as anti-Semitic, obsessed with the notion of Hungarian racial purity.[†]

As mentioned earlier, the *Nyilaskeresztes* had come to power in October 1944 with the help of Nazi Germany. Alarmed by the manoeuvrings of Hungary's Regent, Admiral Horthy, who was desperate to extricate Hungary from the War now that an eventual German defeat was inevitable, Hitler decided to depose Horthy and establish a radical right-wing administration in his place. The success of the *Nyilas* coup precipitated a wave of anti-Semitic assaults by *Nyilas* thugs. Within days, several hundred Jews were murdered and thousands of Jewish homes in Budapest were ransacked and looted.[47]

---

† Szálasi considered himself '*a*-Semitic' rather than *anti*-Semitic, a distinction that was largely lost on the thousands of Jews who were terrorised and murdered by his regime.

Why my great-uncle Ágoston owed his life to football

With the exception of Jews serving in auxiliary labour battalions, others who had gone into hiding, and some living under an assumed identity, there were by this point no Jews left anywhere in Hungary apart from Budapest. Like Tódor and Ilona, my mother's uncle and aunt in Balatonfüred, almost the entire Jewish population of the provinces and the annexed territories had been methodically rounded up during the previous spring and early summer.[48] Held for days or weeks in overcrowded ghettos — often with inadequate provision of food, water, and sanitation and subject to the sadistic whims and predations of their Hungarian guards — they had been transported to Auschwitz-Birkenau in goods wagons. Out of almost 440,000 Hungarian Jews sent to Auschwitz, nearly three quarters died.[49] Budapest's Jews narrowly avoided the same fate when Horthy halted the deportations in early July 1944 in response to mounting pressure from the Vatican and from the leaders of Allied and neutral states.[†]

'My family converted to the Catholic faith in 1938 and we changed our name from Klein to Kővári,' Edit says, with a chuckle. 'But, in the end, none of that helped.' Despite baptismal certificates and a new surname, Edit and her parents were classified as Jews, in accordance with Hungary's sweeping anti-Jewish laws, and subjected to a raft of restrictions that gradually impacted on almost every aspect of their lives.

[†] While Horthy ordered a cessation of further collaboration with Germany regarding the deportation of Budapest's Jews, he did not threaten to oppose any measures that Germany might take *unilaterally*. In practice though, the Germans lacked sufficient manpower and resources in Hungary to proceed with the deportations without extensive assistance from Hungarian gendarmes, civil servants, railway workers etc. See Ungváry, *Horthy Miklós*, 184-99.

Until late in the War, Edit and her parents had considered themselves fortunate. Like many Jewish business owners in Hungary, who feared that their assets would be expropriated or rendered valueless by anti-Jewish measures, Edit's father had transferred his properties in good time to a trusted gentile associate. It was agreed between them that Edit's family would receive regular, monthly payments from the new owner and that the assets would be promptly returned to the family after the conclusion of the War and once Hungary's anti-Jewish legislation had been revoked.

In June 1944, when over 170,000 Jews had to vacate their apartments in Budapest and move into cramped accommodation in the so-called 'star houses', Edit's family once again thought that they'd been lucky. The building at 12 Hunyadi *tér*, in which Edit and her parents occupied a comfortable two-room flat, had been declared a star house. Unlike most of the capital's Jews, the family could continue to live in their own home, surrounded by their furniture and personal belongings. However, everything changed as a result of the *Nyilas* coup.

'The Death's Head Legion occupied premises at 35 Vörösmarty *utca*, just a short distance from our apartment building,' Edit tells me. 'The Legion had a really bad reputation. They were worse than the *Nyilas*!'

Known in Hungarian as the *Halálfejes Légió*, the Legion was a radical right-wing paramilitary formation. With its trademark death's head insignia, the Legion inspired particular dread amongst Jews and other 'enemies' of the new regime.

'A unit of the Death's Head Legion turned up at our building, in November, several weeks after the Arrow Cross coup,' Edit continues. 'At the time my father wasn't living with us. He was in Budapest but he'd been called up and was attached to one of the military hospitals as an auxiliary labour serviceman.'

'What happened?' I ask.

'The legionnaires ordered everyone to assemble outside in the courtyard. It was a star house, so they knew that the people living there must be Jews.'

While the other residents hurried to comply with the shouted orders of the legionnaires, Edit and her mother made their escape. 'We took advantage of the general confusion and slipped into a tailor's workshop that was located in the courtyard,' Edit tells me. 'The tailor, Uncle Zoli, was a friend of my father's. They were both members of the outlawed Social Democratic Party.'

Passing quickly through the tailor's premises, under Zoli's anxious gaze, mother and daughter left through another door that opened directly onto the street — only to find themselves face to face with three legionnaires.

'What did you do?'

'My mother didn't hesitate, not even for a moment,' Edit recalls. 'She calmly reached into her handbag and took out a wad of banknotes, holding it out to the men. One of the legionnaires took the money, slipping it into his greatcoat pocket. They didn't say anything, but they moved aside to let us pass.'

'Where did you go?'

'There was a big green building, a public convenience, right across the road from where we were standing,' Edit recalls. 'We made straight for it. That lavatory became our home for the next three days and nights. That's when I learnt that wrapping yourself in newspapers is a good way to keep warm.'

Known as Beetz conveniences, after the name of the company that built them, the ornate green public lavatories first appeared in Budapest in 1895. By the outbreak of

World War Two, there were eighty-two Beetz conveniences located at various points in the city.

'My mother gave all of her remaining money to the lavatory attendant, who promised to find my father and tell him where we were hiding,' Edit recalls. 'My mother knew that he was in Budapest and that he'd been posted to the Róbert Károly Hospital.'

After some perilous months stationed in Rakhiv, in occupied Soviet territory, Edit's father — drawing on all of his legendary charm and persuasiveness — had managed to get himself transferred to Budapest. Although still a labour conscript, he had obtained a safe and privileged assignment as the personal driver of the hospital's director. For the duration of the War, the Róbert Károly Hospital was placed under military jurisdiction; its director was a middle-ranking army officer.

'It must have been awful for you and your mother, having to spend several days and nights in a public convenience,' I suggest.

Edit smiles. 'I was just a child, but it must have been nerve-wracking for my mother. Every time someone came to use the lavatory, we had to dash into one of the cubicles. Worst of all, my mother couldn't be certain that the attendant would keep her word. She might just as easily have denounced us to the police or to the Arrow Cross.'

After what must have seemed an agonisingly long time, Edit's father suddenly appeared at the public convenience, dressed in a military uniform and without even an armband to indicate that he was Jewish. 'The hospital director was a decent and humane man,' Edit says. 'He didn't want my father to get into difficulties because he could be identified as a Jew.'

With the director's jeep at his disposal, Edit's father drove his wife to one of the Bauhaus apartment buildings on Pozsonyi *út*, adjacent to St. István Park. The building, which was under the formal protection of the Swiss legation, was part of the 'international' ghetto. Since learning of his family's plight, Edit's father had arranged accommodation for his wife in one of the overcrowded apartments and, through contacts in the banned Social Democratic Party, all necessary personal documents.

'I was desperate to remain with my mother, but my father had other plans,' Edit says, with a wry smile. 'He took me to an apartment in another part of the city. It had been turned into a Jewish orphanage, with somewhere between fifteen and twenty children. My father thought I'd be safe there.' Edit pauses, recalling events from over seventy years ago that are indelibly imprinted on her mind. 'If I hadn't been a naughty child I wouldn't be alive now!' she tells me. 'I really hated that orphanage. After a day or two, I managed to escape. I went straight to Uncle Zoli and he took me to my mother.'

As the siege of Budapest intensified, *Nyilas* militiamen raided the Jewish orphanage to which Edit had been taken by her father. 'Later, I heard that the *Nyilas* ordered all the staff and children to accompany them,' Edit says. 'I don't know where they took them, but no one survived. If I hadn't escaped, I'd be dead too.'

As I began to write a preliminary draft of this chapter, I realised that Edit's account of her wartime experiences, which I had recorded in 2015, was incomplete. Where was the orphanage situated? Edit must have known the apartment's approximate location, even if she couldn't remember the name of the street. But it was too late. I could no longer pick up the phone and ask her, or arrange to meet her for a *hosszú lépés* or white wine spritzer at the Piccolo, the tiny, old fashioned bar on Pozsonyi *út* that we both frequented.

In March 2020, at the age of 83, Edit, a recklessly heavy smoker, had succumbed to lung cancer.

Perhaps Edit had been taken by her father to the Jewish children's home situated on Vilma Királynő *út*? On Christmas Day, 1944, a *Nyilas* squad had raided the orphanage shooting and killing a nine-year-old girl and an older boy, before ordering the remaining children to accompany them to the banks of the Danube. Most of the orphans managed to run away when an air raid forced the militiamen to take cover. Even so, the *Nyilas* managed to shoot three of the children and one of their teachers, throwing the bodies into the Danube.[50]

Or maybe Edit had briefly stayed at the Jewish orphanage on Munkácsy Mihály *utca*? On Christmas Eve, 1944, a *Nyilas* unit had turned up at the orphanage, ordering everyone to assemble outside in the courtyard. Five people who were subsequently discovered inside the building, including a toddler aged eighteen months, a child of three, and a care assistant, were summarily shot.[51] The orphanage's remaining residents were ordered to accompany the militiamen to the Radetzky Barracks. A fifteen-year-old youth, who was handicapped and unable to keep up, was shot.

In late December 1944, as the Red Army gradually overcame fierce resistance in Budapest from German troops and their Hungarian allies, Soviet soldiers burst into the basement of an apartment building in Pest. Amongst the civilians huddled there, in the semi-darkness, were Edit and her parents. Fleeing the international ghetto during a *Nyilas* raid, Edit and her mother had been given shelter in the apartment of a family who would have been shocked to discover that they were Jews. The family, who'd been assured by Edit's father that the women were Hungarian refugees from Transylvania, hired Edit's mother as a live-in maid, allowing Edit to live with them too.

Fearing retribution because of their ties to prominent Arrow Cross figures, the family disappeared without warning shortly before the collapse of armed resistance in Pest. Soon afterwards, Edit's father deserted his post at the Róbert Károly Hospital, joining his wife and daughter in the apartment for the final, climactic days of the siege.

17

Sugar beet and szalonna

Y ou're not a Jew!' snaps my mother, with a sudden and unexpected rush of anger. For an instant I'm confused, uncertain what to say or what to think. Was I adopted? Have I been the victim of an elaborate though well-intentioned deception like Miklós Radnóti? The poet discovered at the age of twelve that the woman he had always known as his mother was really his aunt, and that his sister was just a half-sister.

Etelka and my mother by the Danube
near Budapest, 1954

'Only people who've lived through the things I've lived through can call themselves Jews!' exclaims my mother, who turns out to have been my mother after all, even though she rejects the notion that we share a common identity. For my mother, history has erected an impenetrable barrier between us. The Holocaust has created an unbreachable wall between her and her only child. I was born seven years after the defeat of Nazi Germany. How can I possibly understand her or her life?

From a strictly theological perspective, my mother's definition of Jewishness is seriously flawed. If widely adopted, her definition would lead to some bizarre results. Applying my mother's narrow, Holocaust-centric characterization of Jewishness, Moses, King David, the Twelve Apostles, the mediaeval physician and Talmudic scholar Moshe ben Maimon, as well as a host of supposedly Jewish luminaries, including Baruch Spinoza, Benjamin Disraeli, Felix Mendelssohn, Gustav Mahler, Alfred Dreyfus, Osip Mandelstam, and the venerable founder of the international Zionist movement, Theodor Herzl, would no longer qualify as Jews. Unlike my mother, none of them lived through the *Shoah*.

Of course, those of us born *after* May 1945, including most working rabbis and the overwhelming majority of the citizens of the state of Israel, would also have no right to call ourselves Jews. None of us went through those experiences that shaped my mother's life and so nearly resulted in her death.

There seems little point in arguing with my mother, or in reminding her of the conventional religious definition of Jewishness. According to the *halakha* or Jewish religious law, the child of a Jewish mother is a Jew. Under the *halakha*, even an atheist or a person raised as a Christian remains a Jew, provided her mother was Jewish. However, the *halakha*, which evolved over two and a half millennia, does not include personal experience of the *Shoah* as an essential element of Jewishness.

Despite the weakness of my mother's thesis, that only a survivor or a victim of the *Shoah* can be considered a Jew, my mother is adamant. After all, unlike her, I have never endured persecution because of my Jewish ancestry. I have never had to wear a yellow star sewn onto my clothes. I have never had to live amongst strangers, with false identity papers, or experienced the visceral fear that someone might discover my real identity and betray me to the police or to *Nyilas* militiamen. I have never had to spend several days and nights sleeping in rain-sodden clothes in a brickyard that has been converted into a makeshift ghetto. I have never had to escape, under cover of darkness, from a column of frightened, weary women escorted by sullen Hungarian gendarmes. I have never had to watch as my lame father was taken away by gun-toting teenagers wearing the insignia of the Arrow Cross. I have never had to wait, with diminishing hope, for my father to return from a destination that was never revealed to him or to his family. Even though I am in my late sixties, both of my parents are alive.

More than twenty years earlier, when I conceived the idea of writing this book, I began to record lengthy interviews with my mother and with Bertalan, her younger brother, then a semi-retired civil engineer living in the quiet, outer suburbs of Toronto. On one occasion, when my mother was visiting me in Britain from her home in Holland, we drove to Chipping Camden in the Cotswolds, barely half an hour's distance from my home. After ordering filter coffees and toasted teacakes in an up-market bistro we settled into comfortable leather armchairs, a cassette-recorder on the table between us

After a little prompting my mother began to talk, although at first she was hesitant and almost inaudible. I asked her to describe, in as much detail as possible, what had happened to her and to her father in late autumn 1944, following the coup that brought Hungary's Nazi-style Arrow Cross Party to power. I already knew that Miklós and my mother had been amongst almost 30,000 Jewish slave labourers who had set out from Budapest on foot to boost the Reich's flagging war effort. It was a journey from which only my mother would return.

Entrance to one of Budapest's
'star houses', 1944

'I was so eager to please,' begins my mother, smiling ruefully.
'A notice went up in the entrance to our apartment building
instructing Jewish women aged between sixteen and forty
to present themselves for labour service the following
morning. I got up really early the next day so that I would
be amongst the very first in line. I wanted them to see how
keen I was to work!'

At the time, my mother, uncle, and maternal grandparents Etelka and Miklós shared a small room in Uncle
Ármin's rented apartment at 36 Kresz Géza *utca*, one of the
fewer than 2,000 star houses scattered around the city, in
which over 170,000 Jews had scrambled to find accommodation the previous June.

Ármin had been relieved that his apartment building, in
the heavily Jewish Újlipotváros district, was to be classified
as a star house. Nevertheless, he was alarmed at the prospect
of having to share his two-room flat with strangers. To
forestall such unpleasantness, Ármin had invited his sister
Etelka to move into the smaller of the two rooms, together

with her family. Etelka's flat, on Szinyei Merse *utca*, was located in a building that had not been designated for Jewish occupancy.

Although conceived as a temporary measure, the star houses had assumed a semi-permanent character after an order issued by Hungary's Regent in early July 1944 suspended the deportation of the country's remaining Jews, now concentrated in Budapest. As recounted previously, Admiral Horthy, keenly aware that Germany was losing the War, had succumbed to mounting pressure from the leaders of Allied and neutral countries, as well as the Vatican. In halting the deportations, the ageing Regent had been motivated by self-interest and by concern for Hungary rather than by a belated crisis of conscience concerning the fate of the country's Jews.[52] Horthy had been anxious to improve Hungary's standing with Allied leaders and to avoid any possibility that he might be held to account for his role in the Holocaust.

'What happened after you reported for labour service, together with the other women from your apartment building?'

'We were taken to the Óbuda brickworks,' says my mother.

'Who took you?'

My mother pauses, trying to remember whether the armed guards who escorted her and the other Jewish women to the brickyard were Hungarian gendarmes, *Nyilas* militiamen, or regular soldiers. She distinctly recalls that they wore uniforms and that they spoke Hungarian. There were no Germans amongst them.

'When we arrived at the brickworks they put us in a kind of hanger,' says my mother. 'It had a concrete floor and a roof supported by metal columns. But there were no walls. We slept on sacking.'

It was early November when my mother, aged eighteen, was taken to the brickworks. 'It was cold, and it rained a lot,' she tells me. 'Because it was open to the elements, the wind blew the rain right into the hanger. Before long, we were soaked through, although we tried to huddle together for warmth.'

My mother has dropped her voice as if afraid that she might be overheard, that the terrible secret of her Jewishness, the secret that she has guarded so carefully for most of her adult life, may finally be discovered through a momentary lapse of vigilance. In her fear of being overheard, my mother seems oblivious to the fact that no one else in this Cotswolds bistro is likely to speak Hungarian, our personal, almost unbreakable code.

'There was nowhere to wash and there were no toilets,' my mother adds. 'They didn't even give us any work to do. The guards decided when we could leave the hanger to relieve ourselves. We had to do it in the open, even though there were a lot of Jewish men held at the brick factory too.'

'Did they issue you with uniforms?'

'We wore whatever clothes we'd come in,' says my mother. 'I was wearing these ankle length shoes. They were the only shoes I had. The soles were coming away, so my mother had tried to secure them with string.'

After two or three days at the brickworks, my mother, together with several hundred Jewish women, was led away on foot by Hungarian gendarmes mounted on horses.

'Did the gendarmes tell you that you were going to Germany to work?'

'They told us nothing, nothing at all.'

Historians' accounts of the 'death marches' that began in November 1944, involving tens of thousands of Budapest's Jews, make for harrowing reading. Randolph Braham has written that, 'the Jews were neither fed nor housed *en route*' and that 'the marches were so horribly barbaric that the route became a veritable highway of death that shocked not only the observers from the neutral countries and the International Red Cross, but also some top Hungarian police and German SS officials'.[53]

In his *History of the Destruction of the European Jews*, Raul Hilberg records that, 'without food, the slave laborers walked over a hundred miles in snow, rain, and sleet to Austria'.[54] Hilberg relates that *Obergruppenführer* Jüttner, head of the SS Operational Main Office, was travelling from Austria to Budapest by car when he passed a column of Jews who were being led on foot in the opposite direction: 'most of the trekkers, so far as he could see, were women. As the car made its way past the marching people, Jüttner noticed exhausted men and women in the ditches'.[55]

In addition to scholarly texts, we have the testimony of diplomats from neutral countries who observed, at first hand, the pitiful state of the Jews sent on these marches. Raoul Wallenberg, a Secretary at the Swedish Embassy in Budapest, wrote a long and detailed note to Hungary's Foreign Ministry describing what he and a fellow Swedish diplomat, Per Anger, witnessed on the road leading to the border on 23 and 24 November 1944. Wallenberg's note is worth quoting at length:[56]

Amongst the marchers there were a large number of people aged between sixty and seventy, people who were seriously ill, people afflicted with polio etc; children aged between ten and fourteen, a dwarf, an Aryan woman, people without shoes, people whose belongings had been taken from them by the Arrow Cross at the Újlaki Brick Factory, people whose papers or travel documents, entitling them to settle abroad, had been destroyed either at the Újlaki Brick Factory or elsewhere.

Many marchers allege that, throughout the entire journey, they hadn't eaten properly and that they hadn't been able to sleep or wash… On 23 November, seven people died at Mosonmagyaróvár and another seven on 24 November. Two days earlier, a diplomat counted forty-two corpses on the highway.

Edmund Veesenmayer, the Reich plenipotentiary in Hungary, reported to his superiors in Berlin that, by 13 November, a total of 27,000 Jews from Budapest, men and women, had set out on foot for the border. Just over a week later, Ferenc Szálasi ordered a halt to the operation, ostensibly out of concern at 'the death rate of the Jewish women'.[57] In reality, he hoped that this act of clemency would secure formal recognition for his Arrow Cross regime from the neutral states.

'We began walking at daybreak,' says my mother, recalling the column of wet, shivering women, several hundred strong, who had left the Óbuda brickworks in early November with an escort of Hungarian gendarmes. 'We walked and we walked. It was late autumn and it rained a lot.'

From the Óbuda ghetto, at 134 Bécsi út, my mother says that they were led to a location near Budapest's new airport at Ferihegy. 'We spent one or two nights there in extremely primitive conditions,' she tells me. 'There was no shelter of any kind.'

At first, I was disinclined to believe this part of my mother's narrative. I thought that, perhaps due to the passage of time or my mother's advanced age, she was confused. Why would a column of Jewish women be sent to Ferihegy, which lies on the eastern edge of Budapest, if the women were destined for labour service in the Reich?

The death marches, which took an average of eight days to complete, generally followed a direct, westerly route from Budapest, passing through Piliscsaba, Dorog, Sütő, Szőny, Gönyü, Dunaszeg, and Mosonmagyaróvár. Surely my mother was mistaken about having been taken to Ferihegy from the Óbuda brickworks?

Later, though, I came across a multi-volume collection of documents, *Vádirat a Nácizmus ellen: dokumentumok a Magyarországi zsidóüldözés történetéhez* (*An Indictment of Nazism: Documents Relating to the History of the Persecution of the Jews in Hungary*). The collection was edited by a Hungarian historian and Holocaust survivor, Elek Karsai, with the assistance of various co-editors including his son László, a noted historian of the Holocaust. In painstaking detail, the documents trace the persecution of Hungary's Jews during World War Two.

Work on Volume IV, which deals with the critical period of 15 October 1944 to 18 January 1945, was completed after Elek Karsai's death by his son, a Professor of History at Szeged University. As I began to leaf through this volume, comprising almost twelve hundred pages, I came across several references to Ferihegy. For example, Document 41b, dated 23 October 1944, is a note from the Swedish legation in Budapest, requesting Hungary's Foreign Ministry to secure the immediate release of Hungarian Jews who had been issued with official papers of protection by the Swedish Embassy.[58] One of the Jews in question is identified as Dr. István Szécsi, born in 1892, who was taken to Ferihegy from his apartment at 58 Damjanich *utca*. Another Hungarian national mentioned in the note is Jenő Wohl, who had been issued with Swedish papers and who was 'apparently to be found at Ferihegy'. These documents lend strong support to my mother's account. For whatever reason, my mother and her companions had been marched to Ferihegy before beginning the journey to the Hungarian border.

After leaving Ferihegy early in the morning, the column of women had recrossed the Danube, together with their escort of mounted gendarmes. My mother says that they headed west, eventually finding themselves on Fehérvári út in the Buda district of the capital, a distance of almost 22 kilometres.

'Did the gendarmes give you any food?' I ask.

'Yes, they gave us pieces of *szalonna*'.

Szalonna, which remains popular in Hungary, whether eaten cold with bread or added to savoury dishes, is smoked bacon without even a hint of meat. It's streaky bacon with absolutely nothing but streaks. Whether the gendarmes gave the Jewish women *szalonna* out of a warped sense of humour, knowing that the consumption of pork is strictly forbidden to observant Jews, I cannot say. Although unlikely, it's not impossible that the men acted out of a residual sense of humanity and that *szalonna* was the only food they had to give.

'You can't eat *szalonna* on its own, it's pure fat, and we didn't have any bread with us,' adds my mother. 'We happened to be passing a field of sugar beet and the gendarmes told us that we could stop and help ourselves. We scraped the soil off the beet with our fingers and ate as much as we could.'

A root vegetable generally considered unfit for human consumption, sugar beet is commonly fed to livestock, particularly cows. But my mother and her companions wolfed it down.

'After we set off again the gendarmes wouldn't let us stop even if we needed to relieve ourselves,' continues my mother. 'I approached a gendarme and told him that I had to use the toilet urgently. He just shrugged and said I should do my business as I walked. That's when I realized how bad things were. I tried to escape many times after that.'

'What were you afraid of? Did you think they were going to kill you?'

'No, I just wanted to go home.'

The gendarme's refusal to let my mother stop to relieve herself was far from exceptional. In a letter dated 19 November 1944, Budapest's Jewish Council complained to the authorities about the inhuman treatment meted out to thousands of Jews who were being led, under armed escort, from Budapest to the Hungarian border:[59]

> Jewish children, women over forty and men over fifty, including persons who are infirm or mentally disturbed, are being taken on foot towards the country's borders. Some of the marchers have to complete the journey without food or rest and without access to safe drinking water. In some cases, they aren't even permitted to relieve themselves when they need to and many end up soiling themselves. As a consequence, a significant proportion of the deportees expire *en route*.

My mother owes her life and mine to Anikó, a slight, dark-haired Jewish woman from Transylvania who'd been living and working in Budapest for some time and who'd ended up at the Óbuda brickworks. Quite by chance, my mother found herself next to Anikó as they marched.

'She was a simple, uneducated woman, a few years older than me. But she was tough and street-wise,' says my mother. 'Anikó convinced me that this was going to end badly for us unless we escaped.'

'Were you allowed to talk?'

'No, not really. But it was getting dark and there weren't enough gendarmes to keep a close eye on us.'

From time to time, says my mother, she and Anikó would pretend that their shoelaces had come undone. They would pause by the side of the road and get down on one knee, retying their laces.

'Each time a gendarme on horseback would approach us and shout at us to get up and rejoin the column,' recalls my mother. 'When it was completely dark we stopped to tie our shoelaces once more. By this point, we were almost at the very rear of the column. None of the gendarmes noticed us. When we got to our feet again the column of women and their mounted guards had moved on.'

My mother recognised the street on which they found themselves. 'I had relatives living on Fehérvári *út*,' she tells me. A young couple originally from the *Felvidék* in present-day Slovakia, Dódi and Feri had obtained false papers and were using an assumed name, passing themselves off as Christians.

My mother remembered visiting the couple at their apartment, accompanied by Etelka. 'I was fairly sure that they lived at Number 14, on the second floor. But I couldn't remember what name they were using.'

Today, 14 Fehérvári *út* is a nondescript modern building housing a medical centre. In 1944, the site had been occupied by a large apartment house.

'The main entrance wasn't locked,' recalls my mother. 'Anikó and I went straight up to the second floor and knocked on a couple of doors. But we were out of luck. Each time a stranger answered the door.'

My mother says that she mumbled an apology and said that she'd made a mistake but that the householders had become suspicious. 'They stood there and stared after us as we left. After all, we hadn't even been able to tell them who we were looking for.'

It was pitch dark and getting late. 'I whispered to Anikó that it was too dangerous to hang around and that we should leave the building,' recalls my mother. 'Otherwise, someone might take it into their head to detain us or to call the police.'

'Did you remember to remove the yellow star from your coats before you went to look for your relatives?' I ask. At the end of March 1944, shortly after German troops occupied Hungary, the authorities had issued Decree No. 1240/1944, which stipulated that every Jew aged six or above must wear a 'clearly visible' canary-yellow Star of David sewn onto their outer clothing.[60] Measuring at least ten centimetres by ten centimetres, the incriminating symbol had to be made from cloth, silk, or velvet and positioned over the left breast.

'Yes, we ripped off our yellow stars and threw them away as soon as we escaped from the column,' says my mother.

Exiting the apartment building, Anikó and my mother headed for the nearest railway station, which was in the Kelenföld district. 'I told Anikó that I wanted to go home and that she should come with me and spend the night there.' Kelenföld Railway Station is just under three kilometres from 14 Fehérvári *út*, or about half an hour on foot if you're reasonably fit and know the way. 'We were lucky. It was well past ten at night when we scrambled onto a local train which took us to the *Keleti* Railway Station in Budapest. From there, we could walk to my uncle's apartment on Kresz Géza *utca*.'

'Did you have money for tickets?'

My mother laughs. 'We boarded the train without even thinking about tickets! You can't imagine how crowded it was! I must have looked a mess but I was young and pretty. Anikó and I ended up sharing a compartment with a group of Hungarian soldiers who'd been drinking heavily. One of the soldiers kept trying to engage me in conversation, asking if I was cold. Although he was drunk and stank of alcohol, I was glad when he put his arm around me. I thought people would assume that I was his girlfriend and leave us alone'.

At the *Keleti* Railway Station my mother managed, not without difficulty, to detach herself from the amorous soldier. Accompanied by Anikó, she set off on foot for her uncle's flat, a distance of almost four kilometres.

'We were exhausted by the time we reached the apartment and rang the doorbell,' says my mother. 'My parents and brother had been asleep. They were astonished to see us, but overjoyed!'

My mother says that she slipped off the small knapsack she'd taken with her, several days earlier, when leaving the apartment. 'I still had a piece of *szalonna* in it and some sugar beet, nothing else. Anikó and I undressed and collapsed into bed. We fell asleep almost immediately.'

'What about your uncle and aunt? Did they say anything?'

My mother pauses, trying to recall that fateful night over seventy years ago. 'My uncle and aunt weren't there. Neither were their children,' she says. 'It was a star house, and Jews had been ordered to move to the Jewish quarter, to the ghetto'.

My mother's assumption that Ármin and his family had already moved to the Jewish ghetto, when she and Anikó turned up at the apartment, was clearly mistaken. Plans for the establishment of the ghetto weren't announced until November 29, more than a week *after* the death marches had been suspended and a matter of days or possibly weeks following my mother's escape from the column of women bound for Germany. So Ármin and his family must have left the apartment before the ghetto even existed. Besides, if Jews had been ordered to vacate the star houses, as my mother suggested, her parents and younger brother would have had to leave the apartment too, along with Ármin, Bella, and their children. My mother's version of events just doesn't add up.

I remind myself that my mother, a statistician by training, has never shown much interest in the *Shoah*. An avid reader of contemporary fiction, my mother has read little, if anything, about the Holocaust. Like my father, her knowledge of the subject is almost entirely personal. My mother knows what she experienced herself and what relatives, acquaintances, and friends, those who survived, have told her about what they went through. But my mother has never wanted to read books or attend lectures about the *Shoah*. However much the Holocaust may have impacted on her life — and maybe for that very reason — it's a topic she's shunned. So her confusion about the precise chronology of events during the autumn and winter of 1944, including the date on which Budapest's Jews were ordered to move to the newly established ghetto, is understandable.

Like hundreds or thousands of the city's Jews, it's likely that Ármin's wife and children went into hiding, with false papers and a new identity, after the Arrow Cross seized power, unleashing a wave of anti-Semitic terror. In his autobiography, *A Guest in My Own Country*, the Hungarian-Jewish writer George Konrád describes how, after the *Nyilas* coup, his uncle and aunt, Andor and Gizella, together with their children, had disappeared without warning from the star house in which they'd been living since June 1944.[61] What renders the story so shocking is that Andor and Gizella abandoned eleven-year-old George and his younger sister, who had been left in their charge after the children's parents were arrested by the Gestapo some months earlier.

As for Ármin, despite his age and indifferent health he'd been called up to serve in an auxiliary labour battalion. When my mother returned late at night to the flat on Kresz

Géza *utca*, Ármin was either with his unit or already dead. After the War, Ágoston made extensive inquiries about his younger brother. He learnt that Ármin, a diabetic who was unaccustomed to manual labour, had suffered a massive heart attack while digging anti-tank ditches on the outskirts of Budapest. As for Ármin's wife Bella, neither she nor her children ever returned to the apartment on Kresz Géza *utca*. Undocumented victims of the *Nyilas*' reign of terror, it's likely that they were killed in the course of a raid on their hiding place or denounced to the authorities by suspicious neighbours and taken to the Jewish ghetto where they eventually perished.

'Just a few hours after Anikó and I went to bed we were woken by a loud commotion,' continues my mother. 'A unit of Arrow Cross militiamen had arrived at first light and were making a terrible racket. They were just teenagers, maybe no more than sixteen years old, with Arrow Cross armbands and old rifles. They kept beating a gong and shouting that every man aged below sixty had to come down to the courtyard at once.'

'What did you do?'

'What could we do?' shrugs my mother. 'My father got dressed as quickly as he could, shouldered my knapsack, with the *szalonna* and sugar beet still in it, and hurried down the steps. They hustled him away, along with most of the other men from our building, before I'd even had a chance to say goodbye to him properly.'

'Did you hear from your father again?' I ask, although I already know the answer.

'Etelka told us later that she'd received a postcard. She said it was posted in Mosonmagyaróvár, near the border. She told us that, apart from her name and address, Miklós had written the words '*Vigyázz a gyerekekre*' — 'Look after the children.'

I wondered who could have posted the card and where Miklós had managed to find writing materials? It's true that Jews facing imminent death during the Holocaust were sometimes able to write a final note to their loved ones. Yad Vashem, the Holocaust Remembrance Centre in Jerusalem, has an entire collection of such letters. Perhaps Miklós had somehow acquired a card and a pencil stub during the week-long trek from Budapest to Mosonmagyaróvár? Maybe he'd written a few words, addressed the card to Etelka and left it in a place where it was likely to be found? Miklós may have hoped that someone coming across the card would realise the circumstances in which it had been written, affix a stamp and post it.

But the mystery doesn't end there. Even if someone had found Miklós' card in Mosonmagyaróvár and posted it to my grandmother, it would have arrived *after* Etelka and her children had already left the apartment, telling no one where they were going. A day or two after Miklós was taken away by Arrow Cross militiamen, and well before he and his column could possibly have reached Mosonmagyaróvár — even assuming that he was able to complete the journey — Etelka and her children had slipped out of the apartment on Kresz Géza *utca*, taking a few essential belongings with them. Although it may have comforted his children, the idea that Miklós had sent a postcard to his family was almost certainly a fiction.

'When Anikó and I showed up that night at the apartment, Etelka understood right away that it was too dangerous for me to remain there,' continues my mother. 'Apart from Anikó, who only stayed for one night, I was now the only woman in the whole building aged under forty. I was bound to attract attention. People would have wondered why, out of all the women who'd been taken away for labour service, I was the only one who'd come home.'

Soon after Miklós and the other men from the apartment building had been led away, Etelka devised a plan of action. 'First of all, Etelka went to see Aunt Margit in Pesterzsébet,' says my mother. 'Etelka was sure that Miklós had been taken to the Óbuda brickworks. Knowing that Aunt Margit was a Catholic, without a drop of Jewish blood, she implored her sister-in-law to go to the brickyard and to try to get Miklós released.'

'Was Margit able to accomplish anything?'

'Aunt Margit told my mother afterwards that she'd gone to the Óbuda brickworks but that she hadn't been able to get past the guards at the gate. It would have been obvious to anyone, just from her clothes and her demeanour, that Aunt Margit was poor and uneducated and that she didn't know anyone important. I don't think there was anything Aunt Margit could have said or done that would have persuaded the guards to release my father. They wouldn't even tell her where Miklós would be taken after leaving the brickyard.'

'What did Etelka do?'

'Etelka told me to get ready as we were going to pay a call on Mr. and Mrs. Garamszegi.'

Mr. Garamszegi had been the *házmester*† at 6 Szinyei Merse *utca*, where Etelka and her family had occupied a

---

† Finding an English-language translation of *házmester* is problematic, as the role, which has been rendered obsolete by technological innovations and economic imperatives, has had no direct equivalent in Britain. In addition to performing the usual functions of a caretaker, the *házmester* of an apartment building in Budapest was responsible for ensuring that the main entrance was locked at night and then unlocked in the early morning, much like a concierge in Paris. Provided with a small service flat on the ground floor, the *házmester*'s principal income derived from the modest sums he received for admitting residents returning home after the entrance had been locked. See e.g. Adam, I. P. *Budapest Building Managers and the Holocaust in Hungary*. London: Palgrave Macmillan, 2016.

one-room apartment until June 1944. Over a decade earlier, it had been Mr. Garamszegi who had taken pity on Etelka when she came to view the vacant third-floor apartment. Noticing that Etelka's legs were badly swollen and that she'd have difficulty negotiating the steps up to the third floor — there was no lift in the building — Mr. Garamszegi had suggested that she take a look round his ground-floor apartment instead, which was virtually identical. From that day forward, Etelka had been on the best of terms with Mr. Garamszegi and his wife, both of whom were devout Catholics.

Following an Allied bombing raid that had reduced the two adjacent buildings to rubble, the Garamszegis had had to leave their apartment on Szinyei Merse *utca*. But they'd kept in touch with Etelka, who had moved into Ármin's flat with her family. The Garamszegis gave Etelka their new address, in Budapest's Seventh District, where they'd been allocated a comfortable, three-room flat.

'How could the Garamszegis help your father?'

'They couldn't. Etelka hoped the Garamszegis would agree to help me. She asked them to take me in for a few days while she tried to obtain forged documents and find somewhere for us to live where no one would know us.'

Etelka brought all of her modest store of jewellery with her when she went to call on the Garamszegis, amounting to a couple of gold necklaces and her wedding ring. Removing the precious items from her handbag, Etelka placed them on the table.

My mother pauses, recalling the scene. 'Mr. Garamszegi picked up the jewellery and handed it to my mother. "Madam," he said to her, "Please don't offend me. I'm not doing this for money. Please take it back at once!"'

Mr. Garamszegi readily agreed to shelter my mother for a few days. His only stipulation was that, for as long as my mother remained in his apartment, her presence must be kept secret as far as possible. Neither Etelka nor Öcsi, my mother's younger brother, could visit her, while my mother had to speak very quietly and avoid passing in front of the windows. If the *Nyilas* raided the building at night, looking for army deserters and fugitive Jews, my mother was to get into bed with János, the Garamszegis' son, who was in his late teens. Mr. Garamszegi would concoct a story that János barely knew my mother and that he'd no idea she was Jewish!

'What was it like, living with the Garamszegis?'

'They were very kind to me,' says my mother. 'I was only there for a few days, but János and I became good friends in that time.'

'Did they have enough food for all of you, with rationing and everything?'

'Of course!' says my mother, laughing. 'The Garamszegis were Christians!'

The Russians had not yet encircled Budapest, cutting it off from the farms that provided the city with much of its food. Both Mr. and Mrs. Garamszegi had jobs, while the couple received regular supplies of fresh food from relatives who owned a smallholding in the countryside. 'There was plenty of food!' recalls my mother. After spending a few days in the Garamszegis' apartment, Etelka came to collect her.

'Where did you go?'

'Friends of my mother's had told her about a couple, the Klukas,' says my mother. 'The husband was an artist although I don't think he ever made much money from his paintings. Most of his income came from his in-laws who were wealthy. Kluka, who must have been in his late thirties or even older, was extremely handsome and a Christian. But his wife and parents-in-law were Jews. Kluka was devoted to his wife, who suffered from a debilitating lung disease. He was determined to save her and his in-laws from the *Nyilas*.'

'What could he do?'

'Kluka was too old to be called up to serve in the army,' continues my mother. 'Instead, after the Arrow Cross coup in October 1944, Kluka decided to join the *Nemzetőrség*, or National Guard. Kluka reasoned that, people seeing him in his guardsman's uniform would assume he was a loyal and patriotic Hungarian. That would make it much easier for him to help his wife and her family.'

The *Nemzetőrség*, first formed during Hungary's revolt against Habsburg rule in the mid-nineteenth century, had been disbanded shortly afterwards. However, it was re-established in September 1944, in the final, desperate months of the War. Its duties included helping to maintain public order and security, deterring acts of sabotage, and guarding military supplies.

'Kluka managed to obtain false papers for his parents-in-law, classifying them as Christians,' continues my mother. 'He also found them an apartment in the Zugló district of Budapest, where no one knew them.' By a singular irony, the apartment in which Kluka's Jewish in-laws took refuge had previously belonged to a Jewish family. The former occupants had been forced to vacate their home in June, moving into cramped quarters in a star house.

'Kluka was looking for a discreet and reliable house-keeper, someone who'd be willing to look after his in-laws, who were old and infirm,' says my mother. 'Kluka was introduced to Etelka while I was staying with the Garamszegis. Etelka promised to take care of the shopping, cooking, and cleaning, even the old couple's laundry. In return, Kluka obtained false papers for Etelka, Öcsi, and me.' According to their new documents, Etelka and her children were

Christians who'd moved from Szolnok to Budapest after their home was destroyed in an Allied bombing raid.

'Once we were installed in the apartment in Zugló, with Kluka's in-laws, Etelka refused to let Öcsi go outside, even to play,' recalls my mother. 'She was afraid that Öcsi looked too Jewish. On the other hand, she thought I could easily pass for a gentile. Etelka gave me a gold necklace with a small crucifix and told me to wear it whenever I did the shopping or ran other errands.'

'What about Kluka's wife? Did she come to live with you?'

'No, she stayed with her husband,' says my mother. 'She was very ill. I don't even recall her visiting her parents. On the other hand, Kluka came regularly and he often brought us food. At other times, I would be sent to the Klukas' apartment to collect various items. Sometimes, when I went there, I'd see Kluka's wife lying motionless in bed. I had the feeling she was dying.'

Kluka's wife proved unexpectedly resilient. Although gravely ill, as my mother had suspected, she survived for well over a year after the end of the War.

'It must have been early in 1947,' recalls my mother. 'Kluka suddenly turned up at our flat.' Since the end of the War, my mother, uncle, and Etelka had returned to live in Ármin's apartment in Kresz Géza *utca*.

'Kluka showed up without any warning,' continues my mother. 'He said that he wanted to talk to me urgently. He told me that his wife had died and that he'd decided to marry me. He said I couldn't refuse him as he'd saved my life in the War!'

Despite Kluka's strenuous efforts to persuade my mother that she was under a moral obligation to accept his offer of marriage, my mother resisted. 'I was already dating your father by then. He was a Chemistry student at the university.'

A dejected Kluka had returned alone to Mátrafüred, a picturesque village on the southern slopes of the Mátra mountains, where he'd moved after the death of his wife.

'What about the Soviet siege?' I ask. I knew from history books that the city had endured the longest and bloodiest siege of any European capital in World War Two. For a little over a hundred days, Hungarian soldiers had fought tenaciously alongside their German comrades, even though they were hopelessly outnumbered and possessed only a fraction of the Red Army's firepower. An estimated 38,000 non-combatants had died during the siege of Budapest, whether from starvation or as a result of military action, out of a total civilian population of 800,000.[62]

'Whenever the sirens sounded we left our apartment and hurried down to the cellar,' says my mother. 'We would spend hours at a time in that dismal cellar, sometimes much longer, particularly as the fighting got closer.'

My mother recalls that the German troops she encountered in the Zugló apartment building — who would have been astonished to learn that my mother and her family were fugitive Jews — had behaved with decorum. 'At one point, some German soldiers came down to the cellar and asked us for the keys to our apartments so that they wouldn't have to break down the doors. They wanted to shoot at the approaching Soviet troops from the windows of apartments that faced onto the street.' After their position had become hopeless and they were in imminent danger of being encircled, the Germans had carefully relocked the doors of the apartments, descending once more to the cellar to return the keys to their owners before making their escape.

In contrast to the polite, well-mannered Germans, my mother's initial encounter with Soviet troops had been alarming. 'Soon after the Germans had left, some Red Army soldiers appeared,' recalls my mother. 'They were wild, terribly drunk and menacing. They kept shouting at us in Russian, which we didn't understand, and pointing their weapons at us. They demanded our wristwatches, which they wore like bangles, fastening as many onto their wrists and forearms as they could manage.'

Just eighteen years old and pretty, my mother knew that she was in danger even before one of the Russian soldiers seized her. 'He grabbed hold of my arm and tried to drag me away into an alcove,' recalls my mother. 'Seeing this, Etelka grabbed my other arm and pulled me backwards, screaming for help at the top of her voice.'

This human tug of war, in which my teenage mother substituted for a rope, could easily have ended tragically, with the drunken soldier shooting Etelka and raping my mother, before handing her to his comrades. However, a Soviet officer suddenly appeared in the entrance to the cellar. Taking in the chaotic scene in an instant, he barked a command at the drunken soldier, who released my mother's arm instantly before slinking away.

'After that, Etelka made me lie down on a bench and covered me with blankets,' says my mother. 'Whenever Soviet soldiers came into the cellar, Etelka would sit on top of the pile of blankets, almost suffocating me. She hoped that the soldiers wouldn't notice me.'

Etelka's ruse was successful. My mother survived the siege of Budapest and the Soviet occupation with her virginity intact. 'I had a Jewish classmate who wasn't so lucky,' recalls my mother. 'I heard afterwards that, during the siege, she and her mother had taken refuge in a cellar. Soviet troops came down, looking for German soldiers. They raped my classmate and then killed her. Her mother tried to intervene, so they raped and killed her too.'

18

A hanging

My maternal grandfather, Miklós Faragó is just one out of almost 600,000 Hungarian Jews who died in the *Shoah*. Although it seems scarcely possible, well over half a million people — men, women and children — simply disappeared. According to Etelka's estimation, an arithmetic of despair, more than sixty members of her extended family were amongst them, including her husband Miklós, her sisters-in-law Ilona and Klára, their husbands Tódor and Imre, as well as Etelka's brother Ármin, his wife Ella, and their teenage children Gábor and Ági. Gábor was fifteen when he vanished, his sister two years older.

My maternal grandfather, Miklós Faragó

In January 1946, more than a year after Miklós was abducted by gun-toting Arrow Cross youths, the authorities sent my grandmother an official document confirming that *Nyilas* militiamen had 'carried off' my grandfather, a disabled war veteran, from the apartment on Kresz Géza *utca*. If nothing else, the document indicated that the authorities were treating my grandfather's disappearance and presumed death as a criminal act.

Letter confirming the abduction
of Miklós Faragó

By the time Etelka received the letter, Ferenc Szálasi, self-declared political visionary, former head of the Arrow Cross movement and one-time *Nemzetvezető*, or 'Leader of the Nation', was back in Hungary awaiting trial. In the early months of 1945, when the Soviet Red Army was on the verge of encircling Budapest, Szálasi and some of his closest associates had escaped, fleeing first to western

Hungary and afterwards to Austria, then still part of the Reich. Accompanied by his ministers, his closest advisers, and his mistress Gizella Lutz, whom he would shortly marry, Szálasi established his headquarters in a rustic inn in the village of Mattsee, north of Salzburg.[63] Insisting at all times on the scrupulous observance of protocol, as if he were still the *Nemzetvezető* and responsible for the fate of millions, Szálasi held formal meetings with his retinue and with official visitors in the inn's simple dining room. In an effort to keep up appearances, Szálasi and his consort moved from their spartan room in the *Gasthof* to a modest apartment above the village post office.

Until the very end, Szálasi continued to believe unquestioningly in a German victory. He reminded his wavering defence minister that Hitler confided to him that he would defeat his enemies with miraculous new weapons of unparalleled destructive power. 'I hope God will forgive me for [what will happen during] the final two weeks of the war,' Hitler had remarked to Szálasi, when they met in Berlin in December 1944.[64]

Ignoring the pleas of his devoted followers to flee to the relative safety of northern Germany as Allied armies advanced on Austria, Szálasi remained in Mattsee. On 6 May 1945, units of the American Seventh Army occupied the village without encountering any resistance. When American troops attached to the Office of Strategic Services entered the *Gasthof* to arrest Szálasi, the *Nemzetvezető* tried to shake hands with their commanding officer. The latter pointedly declined Szálasi's proffered hand.[65]

Some hours earlier, Szálasi had sent the head of his personal bodyguard to inform the Americans that he had never declared war on the United States and that his sole motivation had been to fight international Bolshevism. However, Szálasi's efforts to negotiate on behalf of Hungary were pointedly ignored. Szálasi and his little retinue were taken away, under guard, in a US military truck.

At noon on 3 October 1945, a US military transport aircraft landed at Mátyásföld, then the site of Budapest's principal airport. In addition to Szálasi, the other passengers on the plane included two of Hungary's former prime ministers, Béla Imrédy and László Bardossy, and an ex-state secretary in the Ministry of the Interior, László Endre.

In a gesture resonant with irony, Szálasi and his companions were held in specially constructed cells in the basement of 60 Andrássy *út* — the building that had served as Arrow Cross headquarters during the War. With his customary attention to detail, Szálasi noted in his diary that the walls of his cell were damp and that there was a slight leak from the sewage waste pipe that ran overhead.[66]

Yet, unlike many of his fellow countrymen, Szálasi had little cause for complaint. Amidst the rubble of Budapest, anxious residents scoured the city for food and fuel, often bartering the last of their jewellery for meat or a loaf of bread. By contrast, Szálasi was well cared for. Although his diet was monotonous and stodgy, consisting mostly of bread, margarine, fried potatoes, onions, and soup, Szálasi never experienced hunger. He wiped his backside with American toilet paper and sent his clothes out to be laundered, as if he were staying in a hotel. On 23 November 1945, Szálasi wrote in his diary that he had sent thirteen items of clothing to be washed and ironed, including two pairs of underpants, three green shirts, a nightshirt, a handkerchief, and several pairs of socks.[67] Szálasi was supplied with books and writing materials and allowed daily exercise. He prayed six times a day, before and after meals. These were privileges that none of his victims had enjoyed.

Despite his protests, Szálasi was brought before a special People's Tribunal convened in the frozen splendour of the great hall of the Ferenc Liszt Music Academy in Budapest. Because of the failure of the building's antiquated heating system, those in attendance were obliged to wear their overcoats throughout the lengthy proceedings. In an effort to make the judges, the prosecutors, and the defence counsel more comfortable, electric bar radiators were placed on the tables before them.[68]

Charged with war crimes and treason, Szálasi showed little emotion when he was convicted and sentenced to death by hanging. Addressing the court, he declared that he would be vindicated by the judgement of the Hungarian people. 'May God be with my nation,' he concluded.[69]

Szálasi's execution

Szálasi's execution took place on 12 March 1946 in the gloomy, walled courtyard of Budapest's Markó *utca* prison. As it happens, the prison is just a short stroll from the apartment on Kresz Géza *utca* where Miklós had been living with his wife and children when he was led away by teenage Arrow Cross militiamen.

The day chosen for Szálasi's execution was bitterly cold, a prolongation of the harsh Central European winter, without even a hint of the coming spring. In photographs taken moments before he was executed, a middle-aged man in an overcoat and a fedora can be seen adjusting a cord around the *Nemzetvezető*'s neck. The hangman has mounted a short ladder for the purpose. Two assistants, also wearing overcoats and sporting broad-brimmed hats, stand on either side of Szálasi. In comparison with modern executions by hanging, the drop is short, no more than a couple of feet. However, if the hangman and his assistants are skilful, expertly co-ordinating their movements, death will come swiftly from a broken neck.

The expression on Szálasi's broad face, as the hangman goes about his business, is calm, untroubled. For all the world, he looks as though he's being measured for a suit by one of Budapest's fanciest tailors rather than prepared for his imminent death. As Soviet army officers, policemen, prison guards, journalists, and photographers gather in the icy prison courtyard to witness his final moments, the *Nemzetvezető*'s self-belief and sense of divine purpose remain visibly intact. There are no last-minute pleas for clemency, no tears or wrenching sobs, no sudden rage against his persecutors, no attempt to break free from the noose around his neck or the ropes that bind his arms and feet. Szálasi is at peace, consoling himself with the thought that he's dying a martyr's death. As his diary makes clear, Hungary's balding *Führer* believed he was being fast-tracked to Heaven.

If I had been alive back then I would have wanted to be present at Szálasi's execution, even if it had meant taking a day off work or playing truant from school. If humanly possible I would have been there, in the very front row, with a bag of sunflower seeds to chew on, spitting the husks onto the paving stones. I wouldn't have missed it for the world. As Szálasi dangled from the hangman's rope, his body limp and inert, I would have let out a cheer and clapped my hands, or maybe blown a raspberry through pursed lips, a final, flatulent fanfare to speed him on his way. But no one in my family seems to have felt like that. None of them made any effort to see Szálasi off. Perhaps they were squeamish or had more urgent matters to attend to. Maybe they assumed that they wouldn't be allowed to attend. Or perhaps they'd had enough of death and dying and just wanted to get on with the business of life.

I've often asked myself why God was so fickle, saving my mother and uncle but allowing their cousins, Gábor and Ági, to die? Why did He (it's always He and not She in the Scriptures) allow the *Nyilas* to kill my great aunt, Ella? What crime had Miklós committed or his sisters, Klára and Ilona, for which they had to die? I'm not a theologian or a philosopher so I can't tell you why God decided that the right thing to do in the circumstances was to sit on the side-lines reading comic books while all across Europe perfectly ordinary men, women and children were rounded up and slaughtered in their millions. I wish I could tell you that their deaths have an urgent, redemptive message; that out of incalculable suffering something good and worthwhile has emerged. But that wouldn't be true; I'd be lying. Both to myself and to you.

List of Illustrations

All images © Stephen Pogany unless otherwise attributed. W indicates Wikimedia Commons, PD Public Domain.

Part One: The Old Empire

1 Kontler, L. *A History of Hungary*. Basingstoke: Palgrave Macmillan, 2002: 246-59.
2 Molnár, M. *A Concise History of Hungary*. Cambridge: CUP, 2001: 207-10.
3 Lendvai, P. *The Hungarians*. London: Hurst & Company, 2003: 286.
4 Máramarosi Lapok, 6 February 1886: 3.
5 My translation of two non-consecutive lines from Ady's poem.
6 Information supplied to the author by Dr. Szabolcs Dobson, Department of Pharmaceutics, School of Medicine, University of Pécs, Hungary, 9 January 2018.
7 On the Neologue movement see Rethelyi, M. 'Hungarian Nationalism and the Origins of Neolog Judaism', *Nova Religio* 18:2 (2014): 67-82.
8 On the Status Quo movement amongst Hungary's Jews see Lupovitch, H. 'Between Orthodox Judaism and Neology: The Origins of the Status Quo Movement', *Jewish Social Studies* 9:2 (2003): 123-53.
9 Pogány, I. 'Women's work: human rights, gender and social class in Hungary at the turn of the twentieth century', *Northern Ireland Law Quarterly* 64:2 (2013): 226.
10 *Ibid.*
11 Wiesel, E. *All Rivers Run to the Sea*, Vol. 1. London: HarperCollins, 1997: 32.
12 Pogány, I. 'Women's work': 220, fn. 90.
13 Patai, R. *The Jews of Hungary*. Detroit: Wayne, 1996: 279-80.
14 See e.g. Lendvai, *The Hungarians*, Chapter 28.
15 Molnár, *History of Hungary*: 216-18.
16 Youngkin, S.D. *The Lost One: A Life of Peter Lorre*. Lexington: UP Kentucky, 2005: 5.
17 Lukacs, J. *Budapest 1900*. London: Weidenfeld & Nicolson, 1993: 64.
18 *Ibid., 63.*
19 Romsics, I. *Magyarország története*. Budapest: Kossuth Kiadó, 2017: 379.
20 Lukacs. *Budapest 1900*: 153.
21 On the Tiszaeszlár affair see Kövér, Gy. 'Intra- and Inter-confessional Conflicts in Tiszaeszlár in the Period of the "Great Trial"', *Hungarian Historical Review* 3:4 (2014): 749–86.
22 Fejtő, F. *Hongrois et Juifs*. Paris: Éditions Balland, 1997: 154.
23 Letter dated 12 June 1911, notifying Adolf that his request to change his and his eldest son's family name to 'Faragó' had been approved (on file with the author).
24 On Hungary's gymnasiums see Lukacs, *Budapest 1900*: 144-6.
25 Horváth, T (ed.). *A Szent István Közgazdasági Szakközépiskola és Kollégium történetéből* (undated).
26 Kulik, K. *Alexander Korda*. London: Virgin, 1991: 26-7.

27 Stone, N. *The Eastern Front 1914-1917*. London: Penguin, 1998: 122.

28 *Ibid.*, 123.

29 Erdélyi, J. *A harmadik fiú*. Budapest: Turul Szövetség Kft, 1940: 175.

30 Cartledge, B. *The Will to Survive: A History of Hungary*. London: Hurst & Co, 2011 (2nd ed.): 295-6.

31 Tábori, K (ed.). *Magyar hősök*. Budapest: Pesti Napló, 1916: 165.

32 *Ibid.*, 65-6.

33 Fejtő, F. *Hongrois et Juifs*: 151.

34 Komoróczy, G. *A zsidók története Magyarországon*, Vol. I. Pozsony: Kalligram, 2012): 329.

35 Bihari, P. 'Aspects of Anti-Semitism in Hungary 1915-1918', *Quest. Issues in Contemporary Jewish History* 9 (2016): 58–93.

36 Pomogáts, B. 'Az elsodort falu hetven éve', *Tiszatáj* 43:9 (1989): 89.

37 Szabó, D. *Az elsodort falu*. Debrecen: Csokonai Kiadóvállalat, 1989: 355 (my translation).

38 Quoted in Szakács, E. 'Szabó Dezső "Az elsodort falu" c. regényének elemzése — művelődéspolitikai szempontból'.

39 Szerb, A. *Magyar irodalom története*. Budapest: Magvető, 1991 (9th ed.): 494.

40 Thompson, M. *The White War*. London: Faber and Faber, 2008): 1.

41 *Ibid.*, 346-7.

42 *Ibid.*, 343.

43 Information provided by Árpád Kajon and Tamás Pintér, 'A Nagy Háború blog' ('The Great War Blog'), 30 May 2020 (on file with the author).

44 *Máramaros*, 17 November 1918: 3.

45 *Máramaros*, 10 November 1918: 2.

46 *A Magyar Szent Korona országainak 1910. évi népszámlalása. első rész*. Budapest: A Magyar Kir. Központi Sztatisztikai Hivatal, 1912: 36.

47 *Máramaros*, 10 November 1918: 2.

48 *Ibid.*, 1.

49 'Sighet', in the United States Holocaust Memorial Museum's *Holocaust Encyclopedia* (online).

50 Okey, R. *The Habsburg Monarchy c. 1765-1918*. Basingstoke: Palgrave Macmillan, 2001: 394-5.

51 Molnár, *History of Hungary*: 251.

52 Jászi, O. 'Dismembered Hungary and Peace in Central Europe', *Foreign Affairs* 2:2 (1923): 270, at 273-4.

53 Kontler, *History of Hungary*: 330.

54 'Czechoslovak-Hungarian Border Conflict', in the *International Encyclopedia of the First World War* (online).

Part Two: Living in Modern Times

1 Tormay, C. *An Outlaw's Diary* (2 Vols.). London: Philip Allan & Co, 1923.

2 Huszár, Á. 'Nationalism and Hungarian Education Policy: Are the Literary Works of Cécile Tormay, József Nyírő, and

Notes

Albert Wass Appropriate for the Hungarian School Curriculum?', *Hungarian Cultural Studies* 7 (2014): 303, at 309-10.

3 Tormay, *An Outlaw's Diary*, Vol. 2: 38.

4 *Ibid.*, 59.

5 Komoróczy, *A zsidók története Magyarországon*, Vol. II: 359.

6 *Ibid.*, 361.

7 *Ibid.*, 363-4.

8 *Ibid.*, 364.

9 *Ibid.*, 365.

10 Kontler, *History of Hungary*: 334-5.

11 Document on file with the author.

12 Kontler, *History of Hungary*: 336.

13 Böhm, V. *Két forradalom tüzébe.* München: Verlag für Kulturpolitik Kiadása, 1923: 356.

14 Tormay, *An Outlaw's Diary*, Vol. 2: 44.

15 Cartledge, *The Will to Survive*: 311.

16 *Ibid.*, 314.

17 Tormay, *An Outlaw's Diary*, Vol. 2: 214.

18 'Tagore, a város kultikus alakja', (online, at *Balatonfüred*.hu).

19 Kontler, *History of Hungary*: 362-3.

20 Szabó, *Az elsodort falu*: 330-1 (my translation).

21 Interview recorded in March 2006 (on file with the author).

22 On Jewish farmers in 19th Century Eastern Europe, see Zalkin, M. 'Can Jews Become Farmers? Rurality, Peasantry and Cultural Identity in the World of the Rural Jew in Nineteenth-Century Eastern Europe', *Rural History* 24:2 (2013): 161-75.

23 Nagy, L. *Kiskunhalom.* Budapest: Szépirodalmi Könyvkiadó, 1954: 105-6 (my translation).

24 *Ibid.*, 108.

25 The MTK, or Hungarian Athletics Club, was founded in 1888. Although it has never drawn its support solely from the Jewish community, the club has long been closely identified with Budapest's Jews.

26 Valachi, A. *József Attila.* Érd: Elektra Kiadóház, 1999: 70.

27 Molnár, *History of Hungary*: 271-2.

28 Lampland, M. 'Pigs, Party Secretaries, and Private Lives in Hungary', *American Ethnologist* 18:3 (1991): 459 at 468.

29 Cartledge, *The Will to Survive*: 349-50.

30 Móricz, Zs. *A Boldog Ember.* Budapest: Szépirodalmi Könyvkiadó, 1979: 6.

31 According to a national census carried out in 1910, Hungary's population, excluding Croatia, amounted to 18,264,000 persons.

32 Hungary's auxiliary labour battalions are examined in Chapter 15. On the eastern front alone, well over 40,000 Jewish men served in labour battalions attached to the Hungarian army. Rozett, R. *Conscripted Slaves.* Jerusalem: Yad Vashem, 2013: 49.

33 For an assessment of Bethlen's premiership see e.g. Cartledge, *The Will to Survive*: 337-45.

34 Móricz's short story 'Ebéd' ('Lunch') is not yet

35 Móricz, Zs. *Életem regénye*. Budapest: Fapadoskonyv Kiadó, 2012: 313.

36 *Ibid.*

37 *Ibid.*, 317.

38 Károlyi, C. *A Life Together*. London: George Allen & Unwin, 1966: 95.

39 Pogany, G. *When Even the Poets Were Silent*. Kenilworth: Brandram, 2011: 11.

40 The story is available in an English translation by George F. Cushing: Móricz, Zs. *Seven Pennies and Other Short Stories*. Budapest: Corvina Press, 1988: 25.

41 My translation.

42 On the Manfréd Weiss Steel and Metal Works see e.g. 'Csepel Works', at industrialheritagehungary. com/02-Industrial-Heritages/02-Industry/csepel-works.html

43 These lines are taken from Philip Larkin's poem, 'This Be The Verse'.

44 Kontler, *History of Hungary*: 353.

45 The phenomenon of Jews converting to Christianity, for personal or professional reasons, was well-known in Hungary by the turn of the 20th Century. However, it was more common amongst ambitious middle- and upper middle-class Jews than amongst working-class Jews like Jenő: see e.g. Patai, *The Jews of Hungary*: 371-4.

46 On the system of 'star houses', see below, Chapter 17.

47 Braham, R.L. *The Politics of Genocide* (condensed ed.). Detroit: Wayne State University Press, 2000: 155-7.

48 On Hungary's Anti-Jewish Laws, see e.g. Pogany, I. *Righting Wrongs in Eastern Europe*. Manchester: MUP, 1997: 26-33, 82-9. Previously, in September 1920, Hungary's Parliament had passed the Numerus Clausus Law (1920/XXV), prescribing strict limits on the number of Jews permitted to study at Hungarian universities and law academies: see generally Nagy, P.T., 'The Numerus Clausus in Inter-War Hungary', *East European Jewish Affairs* 35:1 (2005): 13-22.

49 For an analysis of Hungary's Second Jewish Law, see e.g. Braham, R.L. *The Politics of Genocide: The Holocaust in Hungary*. Boulder: Social Science Monographs Vol. 1, 2016 (3rd rev. ed.): 177-80.

50 On the *Nyilas* coup, see e.g. Cartledge, *The Will to Survive*: 406-8.

51 The 'death marches' are discussed below in Chapter 17. See, generally, Braham, *The Politics of Genocide*, Vol. 2: 1121-29.

52 Kosztolányi's short story, which is entitled 'Tailor for gentlemen', has yet to be translated into English.

53 Kosztolányi, D. *Európai Képeskönyv*. Budapest: Szépirodalmi Könyvkiadó, 1979.

54 *Ibid.*, 80.

55 Csillag, I (ed.). *Blaha*

Lujza Naplója. Budapest: Gondolat, 1987: 275-6.

56 See horvath-haz.hu/tortenelem.

57 *Ibid.*

58 *Zóna* portions were originally intended for the enjoyment of railway passengers who were obliged to wait while their steam locomotive paused to refuel or to take on fresh supplies of water.

59 Don, Y. 'The Economic Effect of Anti-Semitic Discrimination: Hungarian Anti-Jewish Legislation', *Jewish Social Studies* 48:1 (1986): 63, at 74.

60 Braham, R.L. (ed.). *A Magyarországi holokauszt földrajzi enciklopédiája* Vol. 2. Budapest: Park Könyvkiadó, 2007: 1322-3.

61 *Ibid.*, 1364.

62 *Ibid.*, 1323.

63 Friedman, J.C. (ed.). *The Routledge History of the Holocaust*. Abingdon & New York: Routledge, 2011: Chapter 13.

64 See entries for 'Belzec' and 'Auschwitz' in the United States Holocaust Memorial Museum's *Holocaust Encyclopedia* (online).

65 See entries for 'Sobibor' and 'Treblinka' in the United States Holocaust Memorial Museum's *Holocaust Encyclopedia* (online).

66 Bikont, A. *The Crime and the Silence* (transl. Valles, A). London: William Heinemann, 2015.

67 See entry for 'Warsaw' in the United States Holocaust Memorial Museum's *Holocaust Encyclopedia* (online).

68 'Irene Nemirovsky', in *Jewish Women's Archive* (online).

69 Rothstein, E. 'Ambivalence as Part of Author's Legacy', *New York Times*, 20 October 2008.

70 See entry for 'the Netherlands' in the United States Holocaust Memorial Museum's *Holocaust Encyclopedia* (online).

71 Ungváry, K. *Horthy Miklós — A kormányzó és felelősége 1920 — 1944*. Budapest: Jaffa Kiadó, 2020: 139.

72 On the 1939 Anti-Jewish Law see Braham, *The Politics of Genocide* Vol. 1: 177-9.

73 Quoted in Don, 'The Economic Effect of Anti-Semitic Discrimination: Hungarian Anti-Jewish Legislation': 74.

74 Braham, *The Politics of Genocide* (condensed ed.): 25.

75 Don, 'The Economic Effect of Anti-Semitic Discrimination: Hungarian Anti-Jewish Legislation': 66-76.

76 Cartledge, *The Will to Survive*: 374.

77 The law is discussed below in Chapter 15.

78 Rozett, *Conscripted Slaves*: 45-8.

Part Three: The End of History

1 My translation. For English-language translations of Radnóti's poems, see e.g. *Miklós Radnóti, The Complete Poetry in Hungarian and English* (transl. Barabas, G). Jefferson, NC: McFarland & Co., 2014. See also *Miklós Radnóti,*

MODERN TIMES

Eclogues and Other Poems
(transl. Roberts, J). Szeged:
Americana eBooks, 2015.

2 Ozsváth, Zs. *In the Footsteps
of Orpheus: The Life and
Times of Miklós Radnóti*.
Bloomington: IUP, 2000: 53-7.

3 Ferencz, G. *Radnóti Miklós
élete és költészete*. Budapest:
Osiris Kiadó, 2005: 290-304.

4 Ozsváth, *In the Footsteps
of Orpheus*: 73-4.

5 The text of Radnóti's letter to
Aladár Komlós, in Hungarian,
is available at beszelo.c3.hu/
cikkek/radnoti-miklos-
kiadatlan-levele-a-zsidosagrol.

6 See, generally, Braham, *The
Politics of Genocide*, Vol. 1: 144-6.

7 *Ibid.*, 177-9.

8 Interview recorded in March
2006 (on file with the author).

9 Balogh, B.L. *The Second
Vienna Award and the
Hungarian–Romanian
Relations 1940–1944* (transl.
Gane, A). Boulder: Social
Science Monographs, 2012.

10 Interview recorded in April
2008 (on file with the author).

11 On the auxiliary labour
battalions, see e.g. Rozett,
Conscripted Slaves. See also
Braham, *Politics of Genocide*,
Vol. 1: Chapter 10.

12 Hilberg, R. *The Destruction
of the European Jews*, Vol. 2.
New York & London: Holmes
& Meier, 1985 (rev. ed.): 808.

13 Rozett, *Conscripted Slaves*: 97-8.

14 Braham, *The Politics of
Genocide*, Vol. 1: 369.

15 Karsai, L. *Holokauszt*. Budapest:

Pannonia Kiadó, 2001: 222.

16 'The Concentration and
Death Camps' in *Music and
the Holocaust* (online).

17 Braham, *The Politics of
Genocide*, Vol. 1: 357.

18 Ferencz, *Radnóti Miklós
élete és költészete*: 490.

19 Ferencz, G. '*Radnóti Miklós
Bori munkaszolgálatának versei
és dokumentumai*', in *Radnóti
Miklós, Bori notesz, Abdai
dokumentumok*. Budapest:
Helikon Kiadó, 2017: 5, at 7.

20 Ozsváth, *In the Footsteps
of Orpheus*: 170.

21 'Radnóti Miklós: The Seventh
Eclogue', in *BABELMATRIX:
Babel Web Anthology* (online).

22 Braham, *The Politics of
Genocide*, Vol. 1: 391.

23 *Ibid.*, 392.

24 *Ibid.*

25 *Ibid.*, 396.

26 *Ibid.*, 393.

27 Ozsváth, *In the Footsteps
of Orpheus*: 215.

28 Braham, *The Politics of
Genocide*, Vol. 1: 394-5.

29 Ferencz, '*Radnóti Miklós Bori
munkaszolgálatának versei
és dokumentumai*': 13.

30 Braham, *The Politics of
Genocide*, Vol. 1: 396.

31 *Ibid.*

32 Ferencz, '*Radnóti Miklós Bori
munkaszolgálatának versei
és dokumentumai*': 20.

33 Braham, *The Politics of Genocide*
(condensed ed.): 110-1.

34 Braham, *A Magyarországi
holokauszt földrajzi
enciklopédiája*, Vol. 2: 788.

Notes

35 *Érsekújvár és vidéke* (online).

36 See 'Ágó Antal', at *Official Website of MTK Budapest* (online).

37 See 'Arpad Weisz: the Auschwitz Victim who Helped Shape the Idea of Modern Football', *These Football Times* (online).

38 *Sporthírlap*, 29 September 1919: 8.

39 '*Az egyes bíró nem felejti el a Ferencvárost*', *Fradi műsorlap*, 1985-1986, No. 9: 9.

40 Braham, *The Politics of Genocide*, Vol. 2: 1123-8.

41 *Ibid.*, 1122-3.

42 *Ibid.*, 1142.

43 Lévai, J. *A pesti gettó története*. Budapest Főváros VII. kerület Erzsébetváros Önkormányzata, 2014: 141.

44 *Ibid.*, 141-3.

45 For the text of the decree (in Hungarian) see *A m. kir. minisztérium 1944 évi 1.200. M. E. számú rendelete, zsidók háztartásában nemzsidók alkalmasásának tilalmáról.*

46 Braham, *The Politics of Genocide*, Vol. 2: 1152.

47 *Ibid.*, 1110-1.

48 Braham, *The Politics of Genocide* (condensed ed.): Chapters 6, 7.

49 *Ibid.*, 252, Table 5.

50 See 'Vilma királynő útja 25-27: zsidó gyermekotthon, 1944. december 24.' (online).

51 See 'Munkácsy Mihály utca 5-7: zsidó árvaház, 1944. december 24.' (online).

52 Braham, *The Politics of Genocide* (condensed ed.), *158-64.*

53 *Ibid.*, 188.

54 Hilberg, *The Destruction of the European Jews*, Vol. 2: 857.

55 *Ibid.*

56 Karsai, E and L (eds.). *Vádirat a nácizmus ellen*, Vol. IV. Budapest: Balassi Kiadó, 2014: 490 at 491 (my translation).

57 Hilberg, *The Destruction of the European Jews*, Vol. 2: 857.

58 Karsai, E and L (eds.). *Vádirat a nácizmus ellen*, Vol. IV: 141.

59 *Ibid.*, 404 (my translation).

60 Braham, *The Politics of Genocide* (condensed ed.): 102.

61 Konrád, G. *A Guest In My Own Country*. New York: Other Press, 2007: 73-81.

62 For a detailed study of the siege of Budapest, see Ungváry, K. *Battle for Budapest* (transl. Löb, L.). London & New York: I.B. Tauris, 2011.

63 Gosztonyi, P. *A Magyar Honvédség a második világháboruban*. Budapest: Európéa Könyvkiadó: 264.

64 *Ibid.*

65 *Ibid.*, 276.

66 Karsai, E and L (eds.). *A Szálasi per*. Budapest: Reform, 1988: 10.

67 *Ibid.*, 19.

68 *Ibid.*, 43.

69 Karsai, L. *Szálasi Ferenc*. Budapest: Balassi Kiadó, 2016: 396.

Printed in Great Britain
by Amazon